Copyright Notice

Strolling Around Jerez by Irene Reid

ISBN: 9798653722844

Book Cover

Photo by Irene Reid

Enhanced by Prisma Photo Editor

Potted History

People have lived and farmed in the area around Jerez since the Neolithic Age - from about 5,000 years BC. If you visit the city's renowned Archaeological Museum you can see some artefacts from that time.

As the civilisations from all around the Mediterranean became more sophisticated, it was inevitable that some would expand into other lands.

The Phoenicians
The Phoenicians sailed into southern Spain from the Eastern Mediterranean around 1100 BC, and they named this area Xera. They were primarily traders, buying goods from the locals and shipping them to other parts of the Mediterranean at a healthy profit. However the Phoenicians had other skills including wine-making, and in this part of Spain they found an ideal place to grow vines for the wine trade. The soil around Jerez is white and chalky. It's perfect for vines as it soaks up rainwater and then slowly releases it. It is then of course soaked up by the thirsty vines. The Phoenicians transported vines from what is now The Lebanon and the Spanish wine industry was born.

The Greeks
The Greeks were also great traders and explorers and they landed in Southern Spain about 600 BC, followed by the Carthaginians from North Africa about one hundred years later

The Romans

When the armies of the Roman Empire arrived they were more than delighted to find an area full of vineyards and the skills in making very good wine. They changed the name of the settlement they found here from Xera to Ceret, and they were soon shipping wine all over the Empire. Oddly the Romans did not actually move into Ceret. Instead they built a Roman settlement called Asta Regia, which these days is a little town called Mesas de Asta which lies to the north of Jerez.

The Visigoths and the Moors

When Rome fell the Visigoths arrived from Northern Europe, but they in turn were ousted by the Moors. The Almohad Kingdom crossed the Mediterranean from Northern Africa, and Just like the Romans, they took full advantage of the wine-making industry they found there. They did move into Ceret and it soon became an important part of the Moorish empire. They also changed the name of the town again to Xeres.

The wine industry had a close shave at the end of the tenth century, as the ruling Caliph ordered that the vineyards should be dug up on religious grounds. However the farmers pointed out that the grape harvest also let them produce raisins – a valuable and popular food crop. So the vines survived.

The Christians

The Christians from Northern Europe began the Reconquista of Moorish Spain, city by city, town by town. The larger cities were conquered first but gradually every

Moorish town was overrun. It took many battles over many years, but eventually in 1264, Xeres was conquered by King Alfonso X from Castile. It became Christian once more and was soon renamed again to suit the Spanish tongue to Jerez. In fact the city's official name became Jerez de la Frontera, which translates as Jerez of the border. It was called that because for a long time it was a frontier town between the Muslim and Christian kingdoms.

The city was split into six parishes, each with its own church. The churches are El Salvador which is now the Cathedral, San Dionisio, San Mateo, San Lucas, San Marcos and San Juan.

Under Christian Rule, the Moors who wanted to stay in Jerez were known as the Mudejar, and initially they were allowed to continue to worship in their mosques. The Jewish population was also allowed to stay, and they lived in the Juderia quarter which was walled off from the rest of the city.

Sherry
Christian Jerez continued to flourish as part of Andalusia. Wine was of course one of its most important businesses and Jerez started to hold a fair in September which attracted merchants from as far away as Flanders. The Spanish crown earned such a lot of money from exporting "sherry" to England that a law was issued in 1402 which forbad uprooting any vines whatsoever.

When America was discovered by Columbus, Jerez became even more important as it sits near the coast and was able to supply the ocean going ships with vital food and wine.

When Ferdinand Magellan set off to circumnavigate the world, the provisions placed on his ship included many barrels of Sherry.

Sherry was so popular in Great Britain that British merchants moved into the trade and stayed there, producing many famous brands. Since then, that famous wine from Jerez has stayed a very important part of life and industry in Jerez.

The Brotherhoods

As you explore Jerez and see the number of churches, you will soon realise how important religion was, and still is, to many of the people.

There are many brotherhoods in Jerez; groups of monks who are attached to a particular church and who are named after some particular saint or event in Jesus's life.

The churches are also home to some very sacred statues which are carried by the brotherhoods through the streets of Jerez on holy processions, especially at Easter. The members of the brotherhood chosen to take part in the procession don their traditional hooded costume and guide the statues through the streets. It is a great honour to take part.

The oldest brotherhood was founded in the fifteenth century, but more were created through the years and at the time of writing there are 44 brotherhoods – and some have allowed women to join their ranks.

You will visit a number of these churches on the walks and get a chance to see the famous statues.

Get Ready

Sherry

One of the main reasons for visiting Jerez is of course the sherry. The establishments where sherry is stored, aged, and sold are called bodegas. There are many bodegas sprinkled around Jerez where you can take a tour to learn all about the sherry making process, try a glass or two, and of course visit the gift shop.

If you want to visit a bodegas you should pre-order your tour. With a bit of planning you could try to schedule your visit into one of the walks, and time it to be in the vicinity of your chosen bodegas near your allotted time-slot.

Here are some suggestions:

Bodegas on Walk 1

Bodegas Tio Pepe-Gonzalez Byass

This bodegas was started in 1835 by Manuel Maria Gonzalez Angel and its Tio Pepe is now one of the best known sherry brands.

The tour times and languages vary from day to day. There is also a selection of tours available, so you need to check the website to book.

https://www.tiopepe.com/gb-en/book

Bodegas on Walk 3

Bodegas Tradicion

This bodega not only gives you the full sherry experience, but unusually it also has an art gallery which you will want to visit if you love art. The tickets include both a detailed wine tasting tour and a guided tour around the art gallery. The whole visit takes less than two hours.

If you want to visit you need to pre-book you ticket and select a slot. You can find details here:

https://bodegastradicion.es/en/visit/

Bodegas Fundador

Here is another wonderful bodega. Booking information can be found here, but you will need to call or write to book your slot.

https://bodegasfundador.site/about/

Sherry Festival

If you are in town at the start of September you could include the Grape Harvest Festival. It's usually held on the nearest weekend to September 8th.

It kicks off with the "treading of the grapes" at the Cathedral. The Cathedral steps are covered in baskets of grapes and the priest blesses them. The music then starts and the Queen of the Harvest and her handmaidens throw the grapes into the wine press. Four young men climb in and tread the grapes. White doves are set free and the Cathedral bells ring out.

Once all the official rituals and ceremonies are over the fun begins with fireworks and partying back at Plaza del Arenal.

Horses

Andalusian horses have always been highly prized – they were excellent war horses and much loved by the Spanish nobility. However by the nineteenth century, the Andalusian horse was in danger of dying out from a combination of disease and crossbreeding.

The Spanish put a halt to the export of the horses in an attempt to save them, and by the early 21st century their numbers had increased and they are no longer in danger.

The Dancing Horses

Over the centuries Jerez became a centre of horsemanship, and this is where the Royal Andalusian School of Equestrian Art Foundation is based.

The Spanish Riding School in Vienna is much more famous, and you might wonder why it's not called the Viennese Riding School. It's because the Austrians continued the tradition and skills which originated here in Jerez, and decided to keep the Spanish connection.

The dancing horses of Jerez are famous all through Spain. Do try to fit in a show during your visit.

The park and arena where the show is held is over 2 kilometres from the station, and from the centre of Jerez it's about 1.5 kilometres. If you plan to walk to it from the centre of Jerez, do allow at least half an hour and another ten minutes to walk through the park itself to the arena.

If you buy your tickets beforehand you will avoid a long boring queue at the entrance gate. You can find details on ticket sales and shows here:

https://www.realescuela.org/en/exhibiciones.cfm

The Horse Fair

If you plan to visit in May you have the opportunity to see the Feria del Caballo, the Horse fair.

It's an ancient festival which started over five hundred years ago as a place of entertainment but more importantly marketing of all sorts of goods. It wasn't until 1955 that horses became a central part of the festivities.

Nowadays the fair is held in the recinto, a huge purpose-built fairground. It's a fun affair whilst still celebrating the skill of the horses and their riders. The highlight is the daily procession of horses and wonderful carriages.

Flamenco

If on the other hand you are visiting early in the year, you should consider the International Flamenco festival which is held in February and March.

Flamenco is always present in Jerez, but during the festival the city explodes with events. The best dancers in the country make their way to Jerez to participate. The prime location to see a show is the Villamarta Theatre, but there are more informal shows in bars and halls all over city.

Out of season, you could try the la Peña Flamenca Buena Gente, see page 154.

Arab Baths Hammam Andalusi

You could visit this establishment to indulge in some pampering, see page 158. You can book a massage here:

https://hammamandalusi.com/reserva/

Opening Hours

Mornings or late afternoon is the best time for sight-seeing in Jerez – just about everything a tourist might want to visit is shut in between. So plan accordingly.

Palacio de Campo Real

This lovely old palace is included in Walk 3, however if you want to visit you need to fit the opening times into your plans. At the time of writing these are 11am – 1pm.

Foods to Try

Riñones al Jerez
This local dish is lamb kidneys cooked with onion and garlic, in a sherry sauce.

Rabo de Toro
Other Spanish cities make a delicious tender stew out of bull's tail, but they use wine whereas Jerez stews the meat and veg in sherry.

Gambas and Tio Pepe
Prawns are always available in the tapas bars, but in Jerez they should be accompanied by a glass of Tio Pepe.

Ajo Caliente
This dish translates as Hot Grarlic, and consists of breadcrumbs, tomatoes, olive oil and lots of garlic. It was a cheap substantial meal popular with the grape-pickers at harvest time.

Tocino de cielo (heavenly bacon)
This little caramel dessert came from the monasteries around Jerez, and its closest match is a crème caramel.

Its odd name refers to the monasteries it came from (heavenly) and the fact that it is very sweet and will make you fat (bacon).

Meloja
This is made from honey and fruits and is like marmalade. So you might see it at breakfast time.

Arriving into Jerez by Train

If you are on a day trip to Jerez and come by train, you need to get from the station into the centre of Jerez.

The Train Station

As you pass through the station you might want to take a snap or two, as it is one of the prettiest in Spain. It was built at the end of the nineteenth century. The tiled walls of the interior are covered in colourful images, and outside is also very handsome.

You can take a taxi from the station into town; just ask to be taken to Plaza del Arenal which is a good starting point.

Alternatively Plaza del Arenal lies about a kilometre away, and walking there takes roughly fifteen minutes. If you want to walk take the following route.

Walking Route into Town

Exit the station and cross the square which lies in front of you. There is a line of trees running along the square's right hand side, and behind those stands a very uninteresting line of buildings.

At the end of the square, turn right into Calle Diego Fernández Herrera. You now basically need to walk in a straight line to reach the centre of Jerez.

Walk along Calle Diego Fernández Herrera. Cross the junction with Plaza Madre de Dios. After about another 200 metres you will pass the Bodegas Diez Mérito on your left.

Keep going in the same direction, passing Calle Manuel Yélamo Crespillo on your right. Walk straight ahead for another 100 yards and you will reach Plaza de las Angustias which is nice square with a fountain and statues. You will also find a church on your right hand side.

Cross the square diagonally left to reach the opposite corner. Now continue along Calle Corredera – it has trees on both sides of the street. It's now just a straight walk into Plaza del Arenal – you will see the palm trees of the square before you get there. From there you can start Walk 1 or 2.

If you want to try Walk 3, make your way to Plaza Asuncion from Plaza del Arenal instead. Stand facing the same direction as the horse and rider of the large fountain in the middle of the square. Walk to the end of Plaza del Arenal and turn left. Leave the square along Calle Consistorio. After about 150 metres you will walk into Plaza Asuncion.

The Maps

Each walk starts with an overview map, just to give you an idea of the route.

There are detailed map sections sprinkled through each walk to help you find your way.

If you need to check where you are at any point during a walk, always flip back to the previous map to find where you are.

To help you follow the maps, each map shows its start point. In addition numbered points have been placed on each map. The numbered points correspond to the numbered directions within the walks.

The Walks

Walk 1 - The Alcazar and the Cathedral (2km)

This walk takes you to the Alcazar, the Cathedral, and back to Plaza del Arenal via other interesting spots in-between. **If you are only in Jerez for a short time, this is the one to tackle.**

Note, the Alcazar is only open until 14:30, so this walk is best started in the morning. The Cathedral which you visit after the Alcazar is open all day.

Walk 2 – The Market and some Pretty Squares (2 km)

This walk takes you to Jerez's busy indoor market, the Town Hall, a pretty cloister, and some of Jerez's loveliest squares.

This walk is best done in the morning when the market is buzzing. Avoid a Monday when there is no fresh fish, as the fish stalls are the highlight of the market.

Walk 3 – The Old Town (2 km)

This walk takes you through the narrow streets of the old town to see the palaces and churches hidden there. It is a bit off the beaten track.

The walk includes the renowned archaeological museum. The Museum closes at 14:00 for a two-hour lunch break, and at the weekend it doesn't reopen in the afternoon.

Walk 1 - The Alcazar and the Cathedral

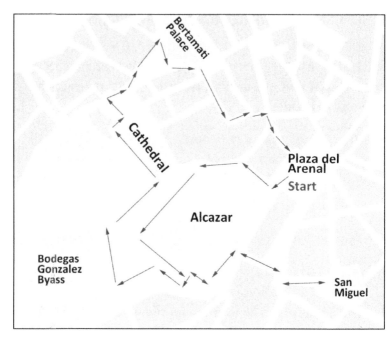

Walk 1 Overview

This walk starts in the main square of Jerez, Plaza del Arenal.

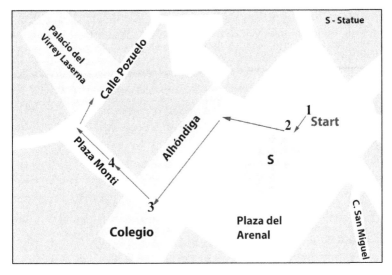

Map 1

Plaza del Arenal

This area sat outside the old city wall which was built by the Moors. It was here that the Moors buried their dead.

Quite recently Jerez decided to rescue the square from the car by installing a car-park beneath it. The cars are now parked well below your feet - you can spot the elevator on the square which takes drivers down to the subterranean car-park.

Before construction of the car-park began the archaeologists were sent in to investigate what lay beneath. Over one hundred skeletons were found – all facing east towards Mecca. Some of them are now held in the city's archaeological museum, but they are not on public display

After the Christian conquest this square became a place where duels and bullfights took place, and it takes its current name "Arenal", from the word "arenarium" which means arena. Those grisly events were often watched by visiting members of the Spanish Royal family.

One particularly long duel took place in the fourteenth century, when two knights fought for three days before King Alfonso XI intervened. Presumably they had some agreed rest breaks! The king called a halt and ordered the knights to become friends.

Other competitions turned into pitched battles between two of Jerez's wealthiest families, the Dávilas and Villavicencios. The two families hated each other and took every opportunity to attack or gain advantage over the other.

Another lively and popular event was the bull-run which happened once a year. The knights drove the bulls into the square and they were then driven down Calle Corredera to the slaughterhouse where they would meet their end. Accidents happen of course, and in one case a bull caused devastation in a church it ran into. All these lively and often dangerous events were very popular and the people watched from every vantage point.

Nowadays Plaza del Arenal is the city's busiest square. It is full of cafes and restaurants and in summer the orange birds of paradise which decorate the garden in the middle light the square up.

Map 1.1 - Walk over to the large fountain and statue in the middle of the square.

Miguel Primo de Rivera

Miguel Primo de Rivera sits on his impressive horse in the middle of the square – he came from Jerez.

He believed that politicians had ruined Spain, and that this was epitomised by the loss of the last of its territories in the Americas at the end of the nineteenth century. He had been in Cuba when the USA defeated the Spanish Army and took control of Spain's last American territory.

Obviously unhappy about this, he led the army to overthrow the Spanish parliament and ruled Spain in the 1920's for seven years. He was a dictator, so he suspended the Spanish Constitution, invoked martial law, and imposed strict censorship. He promised to return Spain to its former glory and his slogan was "Country, Religion, Monarchy" - in other words "back to the good old days!" Anyone who opposed him was either kicked out or imprisoned.

He was a bit eccentric but strangely quite popular with the people – he often visited the provinces to talk to them directly and tell them of his schemes and plans to make life better. He was infamous for issuing decrees after an evening of wine and earnest political discussion in a bar, and then revoking the decree the next morning when his head cleared.

His grand plan included reforming and helping the working classes. Perhaps because the area around Jerez was owned by the great Spanish landowning families and the poor of Jerez were amongst the poorest in Spain.

He tried to raise the cash for his projects by taxing the rich, but not surprisingly the rich were unhappy about it and they made sure that the King was aware of their displeasure. Eventually Rivera backed down - the historian Richard Herr wrote:

> "Primo was not one to waken sleeping dogs, especially if they were big."

So to raise the much needed funds Primo took out huge government loans, which in the end resulted in rapid inflation.

The final straw to his political career was his decision to reduce the strength and status of the military; he lost the support of the army and eventually he "resigned" from office.

Spain has a law forbidding the celebration of fascism, so you might wonder why this statue of a dictator is here. In 2004 Jerez council received a petition to have him removed, and when the statue was removed to build the car-park many thought he would never return. The council however declared that "The History is history" and Primo was cleaned, renovated and reinstalled.

Many believe that the world would be a much less interesting place if its less savoury characters were swept under the carpet. But others disagree, and there is a battle in many cities in Europe on what to do with controversial statues.

Map 1.2 - Stand face to face with Primo. On your right-hand side you will see a long arcade running along the square.

Alhóndiga de Jeréz
The arcade is called the Alhóndiga and it was built by King Carlos II to house a fruit market – but just one year later it was turned into an army barracks.

These days it's a lot more peaceful and it houses government offices and the Tourist Office which might be useful to you.

Walk down the length of the arcade towards the far end of the square.

Map 1.3 - When you reach the end of the square, turn right and walk into Plaza Monti.

As you do, you will see the Colegio Público Miguel de Cervantes on your left – Cervantes's name runs across the top of the building.

Colegio Público Miguel de Cervantes
It now houses a school which was named after the famous Spanish writer, but it was originally built as the Corregidor's

office in the fourteenth century. The Corregidor was a kind of town mayor and responsible for law and order and the running of the town. The last Corregidor left office in the nineteenth century.

The building then became a school for a few decades before the Jerez Courthouse moved in. It was in this building that the infamous trial of "The Black Hand" took place.

The Black Hand

The Black Hand was the name given to a supposed anarchist group in Andalucía at the end of the nineteenth century.

People at that time were unable to find work, prices were sky-high, and the result was starvation. Not surprisingly the people turned to socialism and unions, which those in power did not want.

The police claimed to have discovered a "manual" by The Black Hand, which they said proved that the group was responsible for murder, arson, and other crimes. The result was mass arrests of anyone who the authorities or landowners wanted out of the way. It's said that in Jerez 3000 people were arrested. The court in Jerez sentenced 15 people to death.

This building later reverted back to being a school and so far it has remained a school. The school hall was where the trials of The Black Hand took place. It's said that the tables and chairs in the hall now are the same one used in the trials.

Map 1.4 - Continue along Plaza Monti. At its end turn right into Calle Pozuelo.

On your left you will see an old white building with an ornate doorway and windows.

Palacio del Virrey Laserna

After the conquest of Jerez, the king decided to leave forty knights to run the city. To make things more appealing he gave each of them one of the best buildings in Jerez. Which knight got which palace, is recorded in the archives. They are kept in the Old Town Hall in Plaza de la Asuncion which you will see on Walk 2.

The palace sits on the foundations of the Moorish building which originally stood here. It was given to the Trujillo family, and since then it has been expanded and filled with beautiful items. Look to the left of the arched gateway and you will see an intriguing sign:

```
Conde de Los Andes
```

It means "Count of the Andes", and is an honorary title created by the King in the early nineteenth century. It was given to José de la Serna & Martínez de Hinojosa, who had been appointed Viceroy of Peru. He was a respected military commander who was sent to South America to try to retain control of that part of the continent. He battled and negotiated with the guerrillas who wanted Independence from Spain. He managed to keep power for a number of years but inevitably Spain was forced to cede control. However his efforts were greatly appreciated by the crown so he was honoured with the title "Count of the Andes".

It is a hereditary title so the Count of the Andes still lives in this palace. As you might expect the family has always supported the monarchy. The seventh Count was jailed by Franco because he continued to support the monarchy.

You could take the guided tour around the palace - it is led by one of the family members who will tell you anecdotes about the family and their possessions as you view the rooms and family treasures. The tour takes about forty minutes. Note, the palace closes for a long lunch-break between 14:00 and 16:00. You can find opening hours here:

https://www.palaciodelvirreylaserna.com/visits

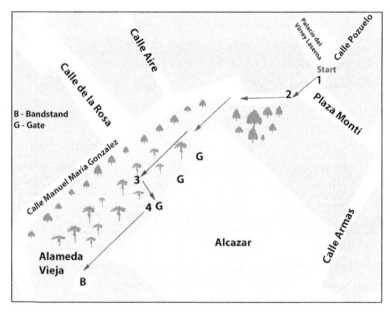

Map 2

Map 2.1 - With the door of the palace behind you, turn right and take a few steps to return to the junction.

Walk straight ahead into Calle Manuel María González.

Map 2.2 - You will pass a fenced off garden area on your left. Keep the garden fence on your left, and then walk up the slope to reach the Alcazar terrace.

The Alcazar is the huge fortification on your left-hand side.

The Alcazar and Town Wall

The word Alcazar comes from the Arabic phrase "al Qasr". It is a fortress where the Moorish military and rulers lived and governed Jerez from. It was built on the highest point of the fledgling city as that is always the easiest spot to defend. From there the Moors built a wall around the city in a rough square shape, with a guarded gate on each side of the city.

When Jerez was conquered by the Christians, they simply moved into the Alcazar and ruled from there.

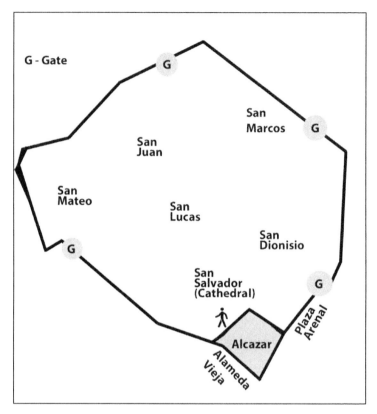

Old Jerez – The Alcazar, the Town Wall, the gates, and the first churches

Much later the Alcazar became the property of the Villavivencio family. They did a lot to preserve it, but the family went bankrupt in the late nineteenth century and the Alcazar was left to the elements. Finally in the early twentieth century Jerez took action to rescue it and a lot of reconstruction took place.

As you walk along the terrace you will see the thick sturdy walls and towers on your left, clearly built for defence.

Map 2.3 - There are now three gates on this side of the Alcazar. At the time of writing the ticket office is reached by the third gate along. However this may change, so do check and follow the signs.

If you are a bit early and the ticket office isn't open, the terrace has plenty of benches under shady trees. You can relax and spot the dome of the Cathedral which you will visit later.

Inside the Alcazar

Once you get inside you will be given a handy little walking guide to follow around the various rooms, towers, and gardens. As you explore you will see many examples of Mudejar architecture - the most obvious feature of which are the many horse-shoe shaped archways as shown above.

Here are some highlights to find:

The Mosque

This is the only surviving mosque from the original eighteen which were built in Jerez – sadly the rest have all gone. When you explore the rest of Jerez, you will find that the six oldest churches in Jerez were all constructed on the site of mosques.

This mosque still has its minaret from where the faithful were called to prayer. The mosque was converted into a church after the Christian conquest and the minaret became the church bell tower.

Inside you will first walk through the ablutions courtyard where the worshippers would clean themselves before prayers – face, hands, and feet. Next is the octagonal prayer room. One wall has a small horseshoe archway which is usually roped off. That is the Mihrab - it faces Mecca and was used by the faithful to orientate themselves for prayer. On another wall you will find the colourful church altar which was placed there during the Christian conversion.

The Oil Mill

Jerez was an important olive producer and here is its huge oil mill which squeezed the olives to extract the valuable oil.

The mill was added by the Villavivencio family in the seventeenth century.

The Parade Ground and the Horse Statue

This open area became a parade ground once the Christians took charge. Soldiers would march up and down in formation to the delight of the military commanders. These days it is beautifully laid out with cobblestones, and it holds a wonderful modern statue of three bronze horses – celebrating Jerez's famous horses.

The Villavicencio Palace

This pink palace was built by the Villavicencio family as a place of comfort for when the family visited, and was built on top of the original old Moorish palace. The main door has the family coat of arms on either side. The large central coat of arms topped with a crown is a kind of thank-you to the king for the family's wealth and position.

You can visit inside. Climb the stairs to visit the eighteenth century pharmacy. It is furnished with the original wooden cabinets and counters, and is stocked with the handsome jars and bottles where mendicants were stored and turned into potions and lotions.

If you climb right to the top of the palace you will find the Camera Obscura which is fun to visit. The operator will use a series of ingenious mirrors and lenses to let you see all over Jerez.

The Baths

Cleanliness was very important to the Moors. Here you see a succession of rooms which mirror the bath complexes favoured by the Romans, a cold room, a warm room, and a hot room. The hot room was essentially a sauna. The room ceilings have pretty star shaped openings to let daylight stream in and just as important, to let the steam out.

The Gardens and King Alfonso.

The gardens are full of roses, trees and flowers and very pretty when in full flower – there are also some handsome art nouveau benches for a little rest.

If you keep to the left hand side of the gardens you will reach an entrance which led to the Country Gate – a gate which gave access to the countryside rather than into Jerez.

Standing beside it is a statue of King Alfonso X who took Jerez from the Moors. The statue was originally placed in a Dominican monastery by the monks as a tribute, since the King gave them the land to build the monastery on.

There it stood until the 19th century when Spain started to shut down and confiscate the property of the monasteries and convents. The statue was then moved from place to place including being placed on the streets of Jerez where it was vandalized. Finally it was rescued by the city council and installed here in the Alcazar.

Archaeological Site

The Archaeological Site provides a series of walkways over the dig. There is lots of information dotted around on notice boards which you can take the time to absorb - if the sun isn't blazing down on you!

Once past the dig you reach the walls and towers which you can climb, the best of which is the Octagonal Tower.

Octagonal Tower

This is the highest point in the Alcazar, which is itself built on the highest point of Jerez, so a perfect spot for a defensive tower, and today for viewing Jerez. It's also the reason that this is where the flag of Castile was raised on that fateful day in 1264 when Jerez fell to the Christian army.

Map 2.4 - When you leave the Alcazar, with the entry gate behind you, turn left to reach the corner of the terrace.

Bandstand and Tio Pepe Weather Vane

Here you will find a little bandstand and in summer you might come across a band in action. This is a popular place to linger as the sun drops for both the views and the cooling breeze.

From the bandstand you can spot the Tio Pepe Weather Vane. At the time of writing, the Guinness Book of Records states it is the largest working weather vane in the world.

There is a larger "weather vane" in Michigan which is shaped like a ship, but it doesn't actually swing with the wind so it doesn't really count.

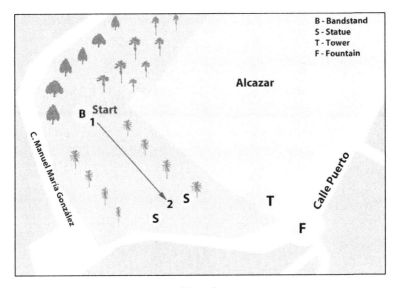

Map 3

Map 3.1 - Turn left again to walk along the Alcazar's second terrace. This terrace is called the Alameda Vieja.

Alameda Vieja

The terrace is covered in pink, blue, and white stonework and is full of jacaranda trees. If you are here in spring you will see them covered in glorious purple blossom. The terrace was only built in the eighteenth century, on top of the moat which used to surround the Alcazar.

Once you reach the end of the jacaranda trees you will find two statues on high columns – they are the goddess Ceres on your left and the goddess Fortuna on your right.

From there you get a good view of the Octagonal Tower which you might have just climbed.

If you have time you might now want to squeeze in a visit to the San Miguel church. It's about a five minute walk away and it is worth seeing.

Note if you plan to visit the cathedral you might as well visit the church as well, as it is a combined ticket for both the Cathedral and the church. However, if you would rather skip the church, then just continue from "To the Viewing Platform" on page 50.

To San Miguel Church

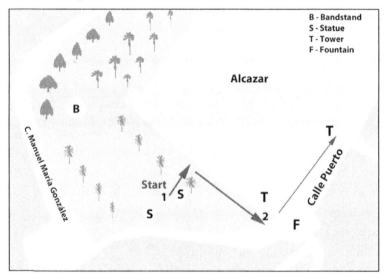

Map 4

Map 4.1 - To reach the San Miguel church stand between the two statues.

Turn left to reach the wall of the Alcazar. Then turn right to walk down a slope towards the Octagonal Tower.

Map 4.2 - From the base of the Octagonal Tower turn left along Calle Puerto, keeping the Alcazar on your left.

After about 80 metres you will reach another tower of the Alcazar.

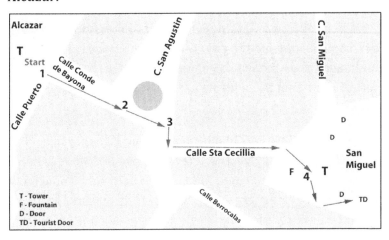

Map 5

Map 5.1 - Cross Calle Puerto and walk straight ahead into Calle Conde de Bayona.

You will see the tower of San Miguel over the rooftops in front of you. Walk straight ahead and you will reach a little roundabout which is filled with trees and flowers.

Map 5.2 – Keep the roundabout on your left and walk straight ahead.

Map 5.3 - Once you are past the roundabout, take a few steps to the right into Calle San Agustín. Immediately turn left into narrow Calle Santa Cecilia.

You will reach the front of the San Miguel church on Plaza San Miguel.

San Miguel

When the Christians were battling to take Jerez from the Moors, legend tells us that the Archangel Michael and Saint John appeared and joined the battle.

When Jerez was finally conquered, the victors created a small chapel outside the city to commemorate the help of the archangel and called it of course San Miguel. They didn't forget Saint John though – he got another church named after him.

In 1484 King Ferdinand and Queen Isabella, aka "The Catholic Monarchs" visited Jerez and ordered that a much grander church was to be built for the faithful. The church took a very long time to build, so it covers a lot of architectural styles. The earliest parts are Gothic but the final parts are Baroque. It has been called the Notre Dame of Jerez.

The Exterior

The church tower is at the front of the church. If you look right to the top you will see that the tower is covered in azulejos, these blue and white tiles from Andalusia. That tower is over seventy metres high and is the highest in the city.

As you approach the front of the church you will see the whole of the baroque façade with its intricate carvings

Look above the door to see the Archangel Michael in warrior garb; at his feet lies the head of the Devil.

Move closer to see the incredible stonework on the columns on either side of the door. The architect was Diego Moreno Meléndez and he is buried in this church.

Map 5.4 - At the time of writing the tourist entrance is round the right hand side of the church, so head that way.

You will pass another very ornate doorway on your left. It has more intricate stone carving.

Keep going to reach the very ordinary door reserved for tourists.

Inside San Miguel

You will immediately be drawn through the eight sculpted Corinthian columns towards the golden altar – make sure you enjoy the amazing star vaulting above you as you approach it.

The Altarpiece

The seven-panelled altar-piece is made of beech wood and took over fifty years to make.

The statues were sculpted by Juan Martínez Montañés who was known as "The God of Wood" - he worked on some of Seville's most beautiful churches and was based there.

Battle of the Angles

The most famous panel on the altarpiece is bottom centre. Here we see the Battle of the Angels, with the Angels being led by the Archangel Michael into the attack from Heaven, and the horned Demons writhing in the flames below.

Transfiguration

Directly above that panel is a depiction of the Transfiguration.

Jesus was in the desert with three of his disciples. Suddenly the prophets Elijah and Moses appeared and Jesus was lit up in a gleaming white light. Disciples Peter, James and John are portrayed watching from below and are suitably impressed.

Ascension

At the top is the Ascension when Jesus finally heads back to heaven 40 days after the Resurrection.

The other four panels show scenes of baby Jesus's life and you can probably identify what's going on in them.

Veronica's Veil – Zurbaran

Find the Treasury room and inside you should find a painting by Zurbaran. It used to be on display in the church but at the time of writing it is in the Treasury for security reasons.

Zurbaran was a Spanish painter who worked mainly on religious paintings and he painted this image many times. His nickname was the Spanish Caravaggio.

The Gospel of Nicodemus relates that when Jesus was carrying the cross to Calvary, a kind-hearted woman wiped his face to get rid of the blood and sweat. She was left with an image of Jesus's face on her cloth. The cloth involved is in Milan Cathedral. The kind woman was assigned the name Veronica, because it means "True Image" and the cloth is of course supposed to be the True Image of Jesus

Nicodemus's Gospel isn't actually part of the bible, and the experts think it was written in the fourth century. Still it's a good story and many artists have tried to depict the veil and Christ's image. Here is Zurbaran's - he has painted the face on a cloth and the cloth is stretched and pinned.

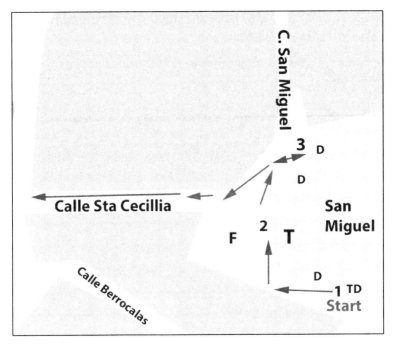

Map 6

Map 6.1 - When you exit, make your way back to the front of the church.

Map 6.2 - Walk past the main door and round the corner. Here you will find two more ornate church doors.

The Good Shepherd

One of the doors is decorated with a shepherd carrying a sheep on his shoulder. It's probably a reference to the parable of the Good Shepherd who searches for and finds his missing sheep.

Map 6.3 – Now backtrack to the square and face away from the church.

Walk straight ahead to leave the square by Calle Santa Cecilia. You will reach a T-junction.

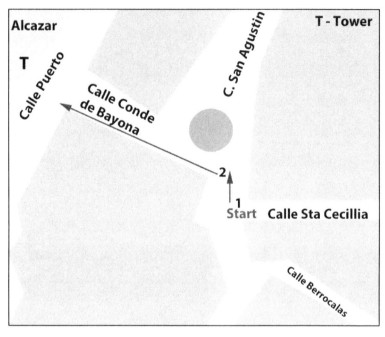

Map 7

Map 7.1 – Take a few steps to the right to return to the little roundabout which you passed earlier.

Map 7.2 – At the roundabout turn left and walk straight ahead, keeping the roundabout on your right.

Walk along Calle Conde de Bayona towards a tower of the Alcazar once more.

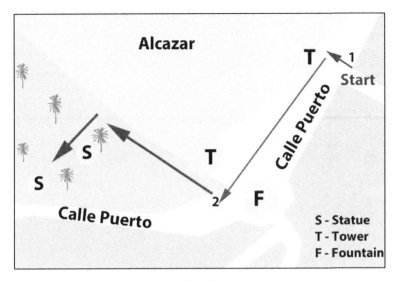

Map 8

Map 8.1 - Cross Calle Puerto and then turn left to walk along Calle Puerto. The Alcazar will be on your right.

Map 8.2 - When you reach the corner of the Alcazar and the Octagonal Tower, turn right to walk back up the slope of the terrace.

Make your way to stand between the statues of Ceres and Fortuna once more.

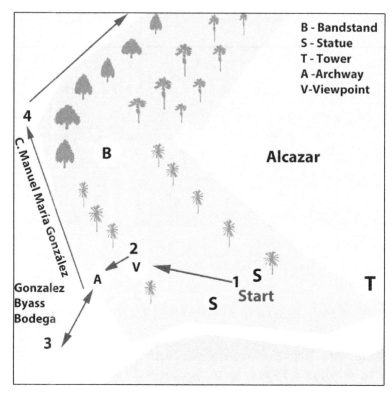

Map 9

To the Viewing Platform

Map 9.1 - Stand with the Alcazar on your right-hand side.

Turn diagonally left to cross the terrace. Go down the first set of steps to reach a viewing platform on a slightly lower terrace.

Viewing platform

It's an Art Nouveau construction made of cast iron which was very popular at the end of the nineteenth century You can climb the viewing platform spiral staircase to see the view in all directions.

Map 9.2 - When you are ready to move on, locate the stone archway which sits behind the trees next to the viewing platform.

Go through the stone archway and down the steps.

Cross Calle Manuel María González diagonally left and you will find the entrance to the Gonzales Byass bodega.

Gonzales Byass Bodegas

This is probably the most visited bodega in Jerez. Check the time as you could join the sherry tasting tour. At the time of writing they run every hour from noon until 17:00. If you would prefer to wait until later take note of where the Bodegas is, and you can return later in the day.

Their tour is very much geared to the tourist trade and at the time of writing, includes a little train to take you to various parts of the establishment!

It follows the standard routine, a tour of the site by a knowledgeable guide who might drop in some amusing anecdotes en route, then a tasting to get your taste-buds activated - the tasting includes "tapas" but don't expect restaurant level nibbles, think more cheese and wine party. Finally you reach the inevitable gift shop where you can indulge your new found knowledge.

The Gonzales Byass Company began at the start of the nineteenth century and they produce Sherries of all types, from bone dry to sweet.

One of its most famous brands is Tio Pepe – it translates as Uncle Joe and was named after the founder's uncle. The sherry business was facing a shrinking market, so the Gonzales Byass Company started an advertising campaign for Tio Pepe to appeal to younger people. They were successful and Tio Pepe is one of the best known brands in the business.

Map 9.3 - When you want to move on, return to Calle Manuel María González.

Turn left to walk along it, keeping the Gonzales Byass bodega on your left, and the Alcazar above you on your right.

Map 9.4 – After about 100 metres the road will bend right, so follow it round.

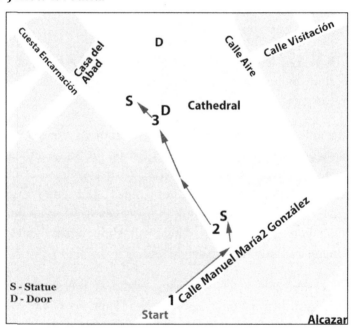

Map 10

Map 10.1 – Keep walking for another 100 metres until you reach a small square on your left. It's easy to spot as it has a statue behind a little railing.

Gonzales Byass Statue

This is Manuel María González, the founder of the sherry company – the street you are on was named after him. Beside him is a barrel of the company's saviour, Tio Pepe.

Behind the statue on the right you can see Jerez Cathedral – its dome can be seen for miles. The dome has a tiny little lantern dome at the top which is covered in very Andalusian blue and white tiles.

Map 10.2 · Stand face-to-face with the statue of Gonzales Byass, and descend the slope on your left-hand side.

It will take you down the side of the cathedral. Pause when you reach an ornate side door to the Cathedral.

Puerta de Encarnacion

Above the door is a carving of the Annunciation, the moment Mary is told about her unexpected pregnancy by the Archangel Gabriel. Poor Gabriel has lost a bit of both arms and his wings look a bit battered. God is hovering above them with the world tucked under his arm.

Map 10.3 · Continue downhill and you will reach a statue of Pope John Paul II on your left.

It was he who promoted the church of San Salvador to a Cathedral.

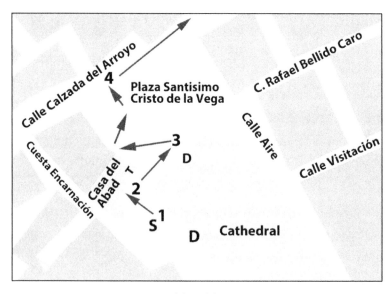

Map 11

Map 11.1 – Continue to reach the very ornate doorway you can see straight ahead. It belongs to the Casa del Abad.

Casa del Abad (House of the Abbot)

The Casa is a two storey building with an intricate stone portal, and it is attached to a tower.

The house has recently been restored, and during those works the excavators unearthed two stone archways which they think are from the fifteenth century. The experts are trying to determine if the house had been part of the original church complex which stood here before it was replaced by the current cathedral.

Map 11.2 - Facing the door, turn right to walk past the tower and around a little corner to reach the front of the cathedral.

The Cathedral

This is where the main mosque of Jerez originally stood, and as they did in so many places in Spain, the conquering Christians replaced it with a church.

Later they tore down the church which was in the process of falling down anyway, and they replaced it with this bigger and better church. It was designed by a local architect, Diego Moreno Meléndez.

The new church took a very long time to build as wars kept getting in the way. The result was that there was more than one style used, it was also very expensive to build, and it took the reign of three Spanish Kings to complete it. They financed it by using the taxes from the local wine industry.

Despite previous attempts by Jerez to have their beautiful church elevated to a Cathedral in the sixteenth and eighteenth centuries, it didn't happen until 1980, courtesy of Pope John Paul II. He was rewarded with the statue which you just saw.

The Tower

The only part of the original church to survive is the tower which you just passed.

That tower went up in the fifteenth century and is thought to have been built on the site of the minaret which stood here. The first section of the tower is in Gothic-Mudéjar style, a mixture of Gothic and Moorish design. Look up to see a typically Gothic flamboyance carving around the first large windows. The tower was heightened when the new church was built and the upper windows are much plainer.

Cathedral Facade

The Cathedral façade has lots of sculpture and engravings, but they have not fared well, and it's probably about time the restorers moved in and applied their talents.

Look below the central window to see another depiction of the Transfiguration - the moment when Jesus is lit up in a blaze of light while in the desert with some of his disciples – they are suitably impressed. Sadly the carving needs a lot of restoration – Jesus is in need of new arms. Above the left hand door we see the Magi inspecting the baby Jesus.

If you are here in September you might see the start of The Feria de la Vendimia - the grape harvest festival which starts with grape-treading on the steps of the cathedral.

Make your way into the Cathedral. At the ticket office you will find a variety of tickets for sale. You have the option of adding a visit to the tower to your ticket. Make sure you pick up the audio guide to thoroughly explore the cathedral.

Cathedral Interior

The Cathedral has five naves. The central one is lined with ornate Corinthian columns – and on them you will find the apostles in colourful garb, guiding you towards the altar.

Look up as you explore to see the richly decorated rib vaulting. When you near the altar the octagonal dome sits high above you.

As you explore the cathedral do look at the stained glass as some of it is quite lovely.

Look to the left of the main altar. You will find an altar which is home to one of the Cathedral's most precious statues.

Cristo de la Viga

It's a gothic carving which portrays the crucifixion, and it is brutally realistic in the depiction of the pain and suffering that Christ must have endured. It is thought to be from the fifteenth century and it is the oldest statue carried in Jerez's holy processions by the Cristo de Viga brotherhood. It is made of walnut and has undergone various restorations over the centuries.

Return to the front of the main altar and turn right. The chapel ahead of you is where the Virgen del Socorro is kept.

Virgen del Socorro

This is the Cathedral's second precious carving. It is from the sixteenth century and was saved from the convent of San Agustin in 1919 when the convent had to be demolished as it was near collapse.

This is the statue, which is mentioned in more detail on Walk 2, where the Virgin Mary turned her head to glare at a rampaging bull and bring it under control.

Note, the Cathedral is also partly a museum, and as you wander around the various chambers at the back of the church you will find paintings and sculptures on display.

Virgin Mary Sleeping – Francisco Zurbarán

You will probably find other tourists around this famous painting which shows a young Virgin Mary having a little nap – perhaps she was bored with her book. Flowers often have symbolic meanings in art as do the little group beside Mary. There is a Rose for love, a Lily or purity, and a Carnation for Fidelity.

The artist has made Mary look like an ordinary person, an approach which was popular at the time it was painted. The reason was that the characters of the bible were said to become holy through their actions; they were not born that way – well apart from Jesus!

Zurbaran was a seventeenth century artist who specialised in religious paintings. His nickname was The Spanish Caravaggio because of his skill in Chiaroscuro, a technique Caravaggio excelled at. It involves the use of sharp colour contrasts to give the painting a depth and volume. It's said that from any angle, the Virgin in this painting appears to be in 3D – make up your own mind.

Map 11.3 - When you exit the cathedral make your way down the double stairway in front of you.

Map 11.4 - Cross the road and turn right to walk uphill along Calle Calzada del Arroyo.

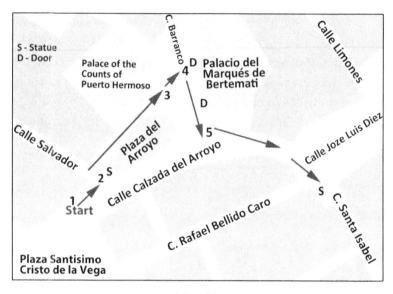

S - Statue
D - Door

Palace of the
Counts of
Puerto Hermoso

C. Barranco

D Palacio del
4 Marqués de
Bertemati

D

Calle Limones

Calle Salvador

Plaza del Arroyo

3

5

Calle Joze Luis Diez

2 S

Calle Calzada del Arroyo

1
Start

C. Rafael Bellido Caro

S C. Santa Isabel

Plaza Santisimo
Cristo de la Vega

Map 12

Map 12.1 - You will soon reach Plaza de Arroya, a little garden filled with trees.

Plaza de Arroya

This area became one of the most exclusive parts of Jerez, but it wasn't always that way. A stream used to run through this area and flooding was a common problem. Not only that, the tanners made use of the stream to make leather which made this a very smelly area.

However at the end of the sixteenth century the stream was covered over and the area became more habitable. The cathedral was built in the seventeenth century and with it came some urban landscaping, and suddenly the wealthy citizens of Jerez wanted to build here.

Unfortunately these days that means their cars are also parked here and this lovely plaza is mostly used as a car park. Don't despair though, there are plans afoot to remove the cars and redevelop the area, so perhaps when you visit you won't have to weave your way through the cars.

Luis Coloma

There is a bust of Luis Coloma at this end of the garden. He was a local author who became a Jesuit priest and was better known as Padre Coloma. He was infamous for writing satirical pieces which mocked and criticised Spanish society.

He is best known however for creating the character Ratoncito Pérez. Eight year old Alonzo XIII had lost a tooth and his mother, the Queen, asked Perez to write him a story. Pérez obliged with Ratoncito Pérez, a mouse who leaves a gift under a child's pillow when a tooth falls out – just like our Tooth Fairy.

Map 12.2 - Face the same way as Coloma and walk along the left-hand side of the garden. The building on your left with the iron balconies is the Palace of the Counts of Puerto Hermoso

Palace of the Counts of Puerto Hermoso

It was originally built for Pedro Loustau who came from France and produced the first brandy in Jerez. He was a philanthropist and helped develop the city's water and electricity supply, as well as being generous in gifts to the poor. His daughter inherited the mansion and married the Count of Puerto Hermoso – which is where the palace gets its current name from.

In the 1980's its sumptuous furnishings were swapped with office equipment and filing cabinets as the police moved in, and a lot of alterations were made to suit their purposes. The police are now scheduled to move out again and into a purpose built complex. At the time of writing the fate of the palace is unknown.

Map 12.3 - Continue to the end of the Palace to reach Calle Barranco. You will see the Bartemati Palace on the other side of it.

Palacio del Marqués de Bertemati

This is one of Jerez's most beautiful buildings. It was originally the home of the Sopranis-Dávila family, and was constructed in the eighteenth century around a beautiful courtyard.

When the family's fortune waned and they needed to sell the palace, they split it into two separate buildings – perhaps because no-one could afford the entire building. The larger half was sold to Jose Bertemati who was a merchant and later became a politician. King Alfonso XIII gave him the title of Marquis of Bertemati.

His heirs later bought the other half of the original building and joined them back up again. When the last of the Bertermati family passed away, the palace was left to the church. It was thoroughly renovated and the bishop moved in. The palace kept the name of Bertemati.

Sadly you can't visit inside but you can see the two eye-catching stone portals. Both have a lovely wrought-iron balcony above the doors; however the stonework on the left portal is much more intricate than the one on the right.

On the left portal you can see a coat of arms guarded by two knights who are grasping the reins of their horses. Above them is a canopy opening to reveal two ladies and a monstrance - a monstrance is where the Eucharist is kept in churches. The doorway and the columns are covered in intricate symbols and swirling stone vegetation.

Map 12.4 - Face the door and turn right to return to Calle Calzada del Arroyo again.

Map 12.5 - Once there turn left and walk uphill. You will reach a junction with a little statue on your right.

María Antonia de Jesús Tirado

Maria Antonia was born in Jerez in the eighteenth century. She fell ill and was near death but made a miraculous recovery after having a vision. She became a nun and had several more mystical visions during subsequent bouts of illness.

Despite her poor health, she founded a Beguine for the poor women of Jerez who wanted to worship but did not want to go as far as taking orders. She also founded a school for needy children and it still survives as a local school. Maria is buried in its chapel.

There have been requests to have her beatified which is the first step to sainthood, but so far no progress.

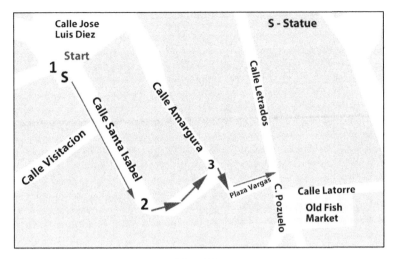

Map 13

Map 13.1 - Stand face to face with Maria.

Behind her find Calle Santa Isabel, a narrow little street leading uphill and to the right. Go along it, passing Calle Visitacion on your right.

Map 13.2 – At the top of the hill Calle Isabel will bend sharply left. It will take you to a T junction with Calle Armagura.

Map 13.3 - Turn right at the T-junction and walk into a little square called Plaza Vargas.

Walk across Plaza Vargas to reach a T-junction with Calle Letrados and Calle Pozuelo.

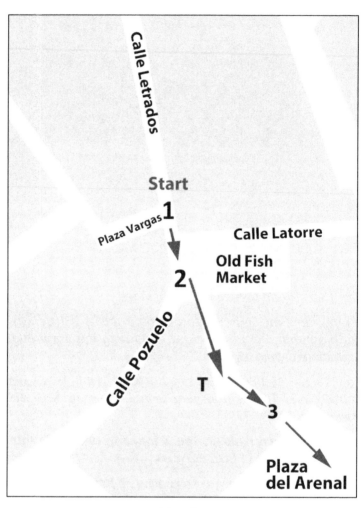

Map 14

Map 14.1 – Turn right into Calle Pozuelo. You will immediately pass Calle Latorre on your left and arrive at the door of the Old Fish Market.

It's easy to spot as it has Pescadería Vieja written above the door.

Pescadería Vieja

The Fish Market hall was part of an eighteenth century plan to fill this area with market buildings, but the rest of the planned construction never took place.

At the end of the twentieth century it was beautifully restored and is now a cultural centre. It's worth popping in even if you are not interested on whatever is on display, as it is full of elegant columns and arches.

Map 14.2 – Stand with the fish market door behind you and then turn left.

Take the next street on your left. It is very narrow and is called Calle Pescadería Vieja.

Calle Pescadería Vieja

The narrow street widens and you will find yourself in another popular dining spot. On your right you can find a colourful tile mosaic of Gonzales Byass and Tio Pepe. At the end of the street stands another elderly tower with a crenelated top.

Map 14.3 - Go through the covered passageway to reach Plaza del Arenal and the end of this walk.

Walk 2 - The Market and some Pretty Squares

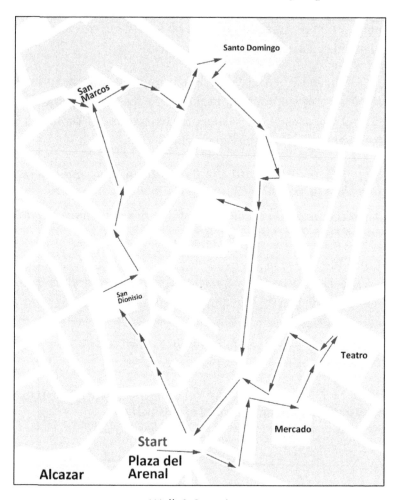

Walk 2 Overview

This walk starts in the main square of Jerez, Plaza del Arenal.

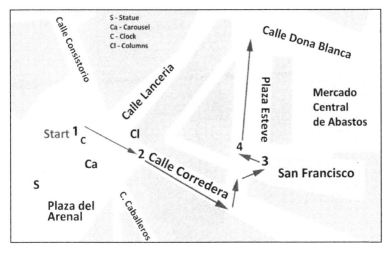

Map 1

On the square you will see a pretty carousel. Hopefully it will be open and running when you visit.

The Carousel

This old wooden carousel has gaily coloured horses going round and round – very appropriate for Jerez. It's a favourite of the local children and is over one hundred years old.

Losada's Clock

Near the carousel stands a clock. It was designed by J.R. Losada who was a famous Spanish clockmaker. You can see his name on the clock faces – and oddly "London".

Losada was a liberal and he fled to London as his political views were not approved of. Once there he became a renowned watchmaker with much of the European nobility as his clients. There are only three Losada clocks in Spain, in Madrid, Morón, and Jerez.

This clock was installed in 1885 when the railway arrived in Jerez. The Railway Company wanted the clock so that the citizens would know the time – something most people were very vague about but which was vital for train journeys. Losada was asked to build it which he did, but from the safety of London.

Map 1.1 - Stand beside the clock with the fountain and the equestrian statue of Miguel Promo de Rivera behind you.

Turn right and pass a building which has four white columns at its door – it's on you left-hand side.

Map 1.2 - Walk into Calle Corredera, and then take the first left into Plaza Esteve. You will find a church on your right-hand side.

San Francisco

The original church which stood here was one of the first churches to be built outside the old city wall. It was originally attached to a monastery but the monastery did not survive - in the eighteenth century Spain seized buildings and land from churches which were deemed to be unused, and where possible sold them off into private hands. The monastery was sold and the land became a marketplace.

The church however did survive but by the eighteenth century it was in a very sorry state, and it had to be replaced by the church you see standing here now.

The main door is guarded by four columns and Saint Francis standing above the door to welcome you in. If it's open, pop in. It's a bright white church with an ornate golden altar. There is a lovely side chapel which has a vault covered in shell-shaped brickwork.

Dona Blanca de Borbon

In the sacristy you can find an interesting plaque.

It commemorates Dona Blanca de Borbon who lived in the fourteenth century. She was a niece of the French king and was married to King Pedro I of Spain when she was just 14 years old. The King didn't really want to marry her at all, and only did so to get his hands on her dowry from France.

Unfortunately for Dona Blanca the promised money did not arrive, and it's said that after their wedding night Pedro returned to the arms of his mistress Maria de Padilla.

Pedro became concerned that his opponents might unite behind his wife, so he had Dona Blanca imprisoned in various castles in the south of Spain, far from the seat of power. She was left there for several years, far from home and any possible rescue.

She conveniently died at the age of 25, and it's believed by many that she was actually murdered by Juan Pérez de Rebolledos following the orders of King Pedro. The inscription on the plaque translates as:

> Christ most supreme and Holy.
> Blessed Blanche, Queen of Spain, of Bourbon Father,
> and from renowned royal French lineage,
> died with a graceful body;
> Common knowledge judges her fallen by her husband Peter the Cruel
> in the year 1361 at the age of 25.

She was buried in the original church which stood here.

In 1477 Queen Isabella ordered that as a queen, Dona's remains must be moved to the high altar. They remained there until the old church was knocked down and this new church was built. Her remains were eventually moved into a small crypt near the altar. So to this day, Jerez is the burial spot of a Queen of Spain.

Map 1.3 - When you exit the church, stand with the main door behind you and walk a few steps to reach Plaza Esteve.

Map 1.4 - Turn right to walk along Plaza Esteve.

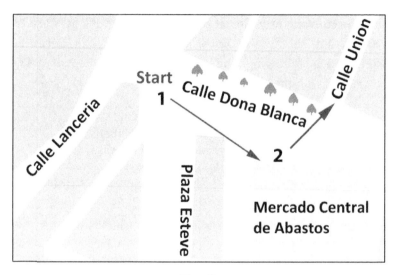

Map 2

Map 2.1 – Take the first right into wide Calle Dona Blanca.

Calle Dona Blanca

This street is of course named after the tragic lady you have just read about. There are stone obelisk streetlights running along the street, and it is lined by orange trees on one side.

The long Mercado Central de Abastos stands on the right-hand side of the street, where the lost monastery of San Francisco once stood. It is decorated with orange and green glazed ceramics.

Enter the Mercado.

Mercado Central de Abastos

It's one of the oldest market halls in this part of Spain and worth a walk around. It was designed by a local architect José Esteve – you just walked along Plaza Esteve which is named after him.

Inside you will pass under the impressive iron archways which were shipped in from France. You will hear the market-men shouting their prices out to encourage sales and find a multitude of stalls in three different departments, selling all sorts of colourful vegetables, olives, fish, and meat – although fish is the speciality.

The prize item is atun de almadraba, which is very seasonable and is only available for a short time in spring and autumn when the blue-fin tuna migrates from the Atlantic into the Mediterranean. The method used to catch them is ancient, using stationary net traps. It does not decimate the fish population like many other modern fishing technologies which simply scoop them out of the sea in huge numbers.

There are cold storage cellars beneath the market where the perishable goods for sale are kept fresh.

Map 2.2 - When you exit the market, make sure you return to Calle Dona Blanca.

With the Mercado main door behind you, cross the square diagonally right to find Calle Union.

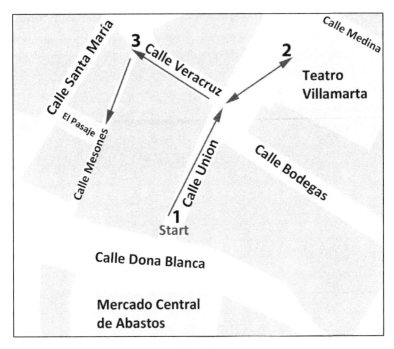

Map 3

Map 3.1 - Follow this little street and it will take you to a set of steps which lead down to Plaza Romero Martínez.

Descend the steps and you will find Jerez's theatre on your right-hand side.

Teatro Villamarta

This theatre was built in 1928 by the Marquis of Villamarta. Stand back to see its two towers decorated with mosaics, and look at the windows in the towers – they are shaped like wine bottles.

It was run as a private theatre until near the end of the twentieth century. At which point the doors closed for business until Jerez took it over and reopened it to give the city a cultural centre once more. It runs a full programme of events, including flamenco shows which you might want to investigate.

Map 3.2 - Return to the foot of the steps you came down and turn right to leave the square on Calle Veracruz.

Map 3.3 - Take the next left along Calle Mesones and find Tabanco El Pasaje on your right.

Tabanco El Pasaje

This is now a tapas bar but originally it was Jerez's oldest tabanco which opened in 1925.

Not so long ago tabancos were where the men of the city might meet for a cigar and a glass of sherry poured straight from the barrel. Tabancos have suddenly become very popular again, and now include tapas and sometimes flamenco in their repertoire. The sherry still comes straight from the barrel but thankfully they have removed the tobacco from the deal.

This one's walls are decorated with colourful posters of bullfighting.

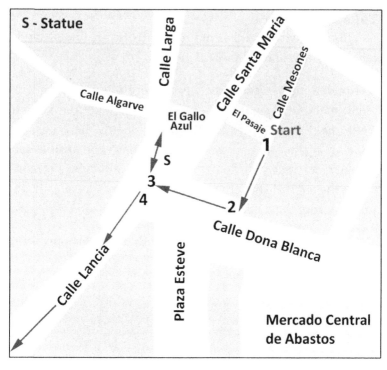

Map 4

Map 4.1 - Continue along Calle Mesones and you will return to Calle Dona Blanca.

Map 4.2 - Turn right to reach Plaza Esteve. Use the zebra crossing you will find there to reach the pedestrianised area in front of you.

Map 4.3 - Once over turn right to see the eye-catching building which is called El Gallo Azul.

El Gallo Azul

This corner of Jerez was in need of restoration, so in 1927 the city council ran a competition to design an iconic building, the prize being the right to build the winning entry. The competition was won by the Domecq family, one of Jerez's sherry families, and this wonderful circular building went up in 1929.

The family then generously gave the building to Jerez as a gift to celebrate the Seville exposition of that year. You can still see the family name at the top of the building, and there is a large FUNDADOR sign also at the top – one of the Domecq brandies.

The potted history mentioned the Muslims who stayed in Jerez after the Christian conquest. They had their own style of architecture which is called Mudéjar. The most obvious sign of Mudéjar architecture is rounded arches – and you can see them on the second floor of El Gallo Azul as it was built in Neo-Mudéjar style.

Inside is an open gallery with marble columns and upstairs a wonderful terrace – there is a restaurant and bar upstairs and a tapas bar on the ground floor which is open in the evening. The building's name means the Blue Cockerel and refers to a painting by a local artist which hangs above the bar.

The Blue Cockerel was later sold to the Ricard family, producers of both the Pernod and Ricard aperitifs. They then sold the building on again to a local businessman who is still the owner.

You will find a signpost topped with a clock standing in front of the Blue Cockerel.

Signpost

In 1934 the council issued another competition for a signpost to stand outside the Blue Cockerel, and the Domecq family won that one as well. The clock has Pedro Domecq's name replacing the clock numbers. The signpost points the way to the cities of Seville and Cadiz, and at the bottom you can see the coats of arms of Aragon, Navarra, Castile, and

Leon. You can get a great snap of both El Gallo Azul and the signpost.

Map 4.4 – Return to the signpost. With both the Blue Cockerel and the Signpost behind you, walk straight ahead along pedestrianised Calle Lanceria to return to Plaza del Arenal.

Calle Lanceria gets its name from the lances that were made here 400 years ago for the army. It is lined with orange trees.

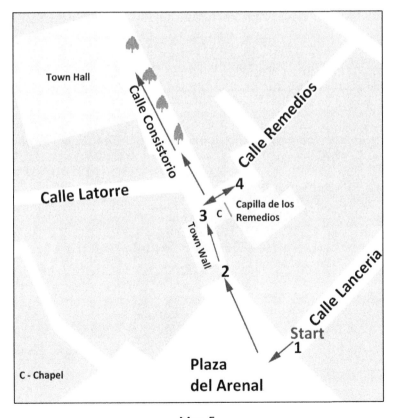

Map 5

Map 5.1 - When you reach Plaza del Arenal, turn right to walk along the plaza edge and you will reach Calle Consistorio.

Map 5.2 - Take a few steps into Calle Consistorio and you will see part of the old city wall on your left.

Puerta Real and the City Wall

This end of Calle Consistorio was where the Puerta Real gateway once stood. The Royal Gate was given that name by King Alfonso X in the thirteenth century.

Here you can see a section of the old city wall which has survived. At the time of writing, it is fronted by a bakery.

Note, Calle Consistorio is a very popular restaurant area, so you might want to do a bit of menu-gazing as you stroll along.

Opposite the wall is the doorway to the Capilla del Señor de la Puerta Real.

Capilla del Señor de la Puerta Real

The tiny chapel is said to date back to the Reconquista when Christian Spain finally reclaimed Spain from the Moors.

In it you will find an image of Christ with his crown of thorns. Images like this are very common in churches and are called "Ecce homo". They portray the moment when Christ is presented to the mob by Pontius Pilate. According to the bible Pilate points to Jesus and says "Ecce homo" which means "**Behold the Man**"

It is a much loved little chapel and in the mornings you can often see worshippers entering to pray. On the side walls of the chapel are personal items placed there by the faithful asking for help for loved one.

Map 5.3 - When you exit the little chapel, turn right a few steps along Calle Consistorio to reach Calle Remedios.

Turn right into Calle Remedioss. Here you will find a more ornate doorway which leads to the Capilla de los Remedios.

Capilla de los Remedios

Look up above the door to see a beautiful image of the Virgin Mary.

Legend tells us that a small chapel stood here and that it held a much respected statue of the Virgin and Child - the soldiers of Jerez would pray to her before they set out to battle.

On one occasion in the fourteenth century the Moors had put Jerez under siege, and much needed help from other Spanish cities had been asked for but had not yet arrived.

The men of Jerez came to this statue of the Virgin, prayed for help, and then set out to try to take the Moors by surprise.

Shortly after they left the city, the long sought-after aid arrived in the shape of an army from the city of Cordoba. Meanwhile the Jerez army stampeded their horses, ponies, and cattle towards the Moors – it was chaos. The Moors broke rank and ran straight into the attacking army from Cordoba – Jerez was saved. The two cities became firm allies and are still twinned.

As part of the celebrations, this church was built and a beautiful statue of the Virgin and Child was placed on it. As you might have guessed, the original statue is now in the archaeological museum for its protection from the elements, and we now see a copy.

Map 5.4- Return to Calle Consistorio and turn right.

Walk along between the orange trees and you will eventually reach the town hall on your left. Its door is topped by flags and above the door is a clock.

Town Hall
It was a seventeenth century hospital which was transformed into the Mayor's office and Town Hall. As you near it you might come across a demonstration or two, as this is where anyone with a grievance in Jerez comes to air their views.

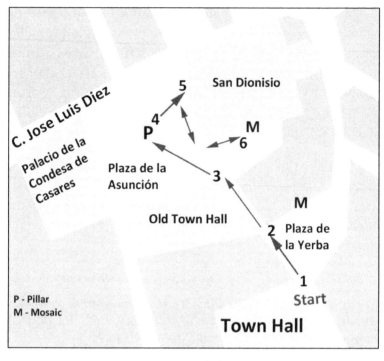

Map 6

Map 6.1 - Once past the Town Hall you will reach a little triangular square with wonderful trees.

Plaza de la Yerba

Long ago the Plaza was an important crossroads between Jerez's commercial, religious, and military districts. So not surprisingly any important processions would pass through.

It was the location of a miracle in the sixteenth century – commemorated by the colourful mosaic of the Virgin Mary which you can see on the façade of one of the buildings behind the trees.

A holy procession was passing through the square and one of the statues being carried in the procession was the Virgin Mary. A bull was part of the procession but it became enraged and began injuring the closely packed people. As you might expect the people being injured by the bull screamed out for help, so the Virgin Mary turned her head and glared towards the bull, which immediately got the message and lay on the ground.

The lovely trees on the square are Jacaranda, the same type you saw on Walk 1 on Alameda Vieja. So again if you are lucky you will see a cloud of purple blossom.

Map 6.2 - Leave Plaza de la Yerba by continuing along the same path you entered it by.

You will walk into Plaza de la Asunción – possibly Jerez's prettiest square.

Plaza de la Asuncion

You are now standing in one of the oldest parts of Jerez. This was where the medina, the old Arab market, stood before the Christian conquest. Later it was called Plaza de Los Escribanos, Scribes Square, because the scribes worked here. It was the political centre of Jerez.

As the centuries passed buildings in different styles were added.

Map 6.3 - Take a walk over to the pillar in the middle of the square

Assumption pillar

In the middle stands the Assumption pillar, celebrating the moment when Mary dies and heads upwards to heaven guided by two angels. Beneath her stand the apostles, each with a halo above his head.

Stand face to face with Mary and look diagonally left to find the old Town Hall.

Antiguo Cabildo (Old Town Hall)

This building went up in the sixteenth century when Spain was the most powerful country in Europe with territories in all known parts of the world. Gold was coming from South America and financed huge and extravagant spending. The wealth and power didn't last of course, but many of the buildings which were constructed during that time have survived.

This is where the city elders met to rule the city. It's classed as a renaissance building, being inspired by the columns, arches, and domes of classical Rome and Greece.

On the left side is beautiful Italian loggia with columns and round arches, and it's a shame we can't walk into it. The right side of the façade is decorated with a statue of Hercules and another of Julius Caesar.

Julius Caesar is flanked by Justice and Fortitude. He was at one time the governor of Andalusia, and he is shown in military outfit holding a dagger.

Hercules is flanked by Temperance and Prudence. He is there to link the city council to the god of ancient times.

The first of Hercules's Twelve Tasks was to kill the ferocious Nemean Lion whose golden fur was impenetrable to attack. Hercules succeeded by strangling the beast rather than using his sword. He then used the lion's own claws to skin it. Hercules stands naked with the pelt of the lion draped over the pillar at his side - he used the hide as a cloak on his remaining tasks.

Beneath those two warriors sit the four Cardinal virtues: temperance, prudence, courage, and justice – all good characteristics for a city council. Above the door is the old coat of arms of Jerez.

Map 6.4 – Stand facing the same direction as Mary and walk towards the church of Saint Dionysius.

San Dionisio

This is one of the oldest churches in Jerez. Dionisio was a judge in Athens who was converted to Christianity after listening to one of Saint Paul's sermons. Jerez named him their patron saint because the Christians reclaimed Jerez from the Moors on San Dionisio day in 1264.

The church started out as a Gothic-Mudéjar church – a hybrid of traditional Gothic design and Mudéjar. However it has been added to and remodelled over the centuries and is now a happy conglomeration of many styles.

Interior

Now go inside if it's open; the church has been reopened after a huge restoration project.

You will be greeted by Saint Dionysius himself – it's a very modern statue which was only placed here in 2016.

The church is beautiful with two rows of mighty columns leading you to the golden altar. The altar was originally in a Jesuit church but later moved into this church. If you look at the columns carefully, you can see intricate ribbon-like carvings running up the columns - those are Mudejar carvings.

Find the statue of Jesus lying on a pristine white bed – the whiteness dramatizes the blood and his suffering. It is called he Christ of the Waters, and it's where the locals would pray during droughts.

The Brotherhood of the Greater Pain

In the fifteenth century there was a hospital in Jerez where the poor were cared for and given a place to sleep. It was funded by the wealthy shoemakers and the tanners of Jerez, and they eventually decided to form The Brotherhood of the Greater Pain. The Catholic Church gave the new brotherhood its blessing and they then took over the full support of the hospital. The hospital closed in the sixteenth century but the brotherhood continued and they eventually moved to this church in 1738.

The brotherhood leads an important religious procession from this church on Holy Thursday, the Thursday before Easter. The procession tells the story of the crucifixion.

Statues from the church are dressed in ceremonial robes and taken in procession around the town. If you look to the right of the altar you will see a statue which is part of the procession, Our Lady of Greater Pain.   Nearby is her ceremonial cloak which she wears in the procession.

Map 6.5 - When you leave the church, turn left to go round the side of the church and into another tiny square.

There is a lovely tiled depiction of Our Lady of the Greater Pain on the church wall - it makes a nice snap.

Map 6.6 - Return to the front of the church and stand with the church door behind you.

Directly opposite the church is the Palacio de la Condesa de Casares.

Palacio de la Condesa de Casares

This handsome building was a palace but it also has a rather grisly past as it was used as a prison by the inquisition. Perhaps because of that it has recently been investigated for ghostly and paranormal activity – people have claimed to have seen shadows and heard screams.

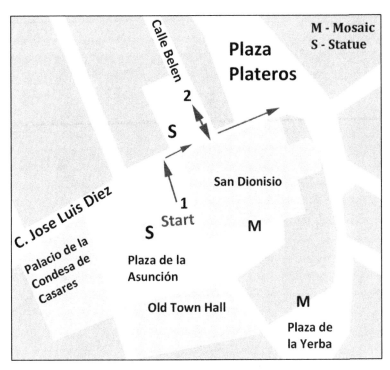

Map 7

Map 7.1 – Now turn right to go round the church corner.

As you do you will find a little square on your left called Calle Belen; take a few steps into it.

Calle Belen

There is statue here which the city of Cordoba presented to Jerez in 1964. You will remember that the two cities were great allies during the Reconquista. The statue celebrates the 700th anniversary of the Christian conquest of Jerez. It's a replica of a statue in Cordoba and it has an inscription:

Córdoba a Jerez 1964

Map 7.2 - Back track out of Calle Belen, and then turn left to continue along the side of the church. You will enter Plaza Plateros.

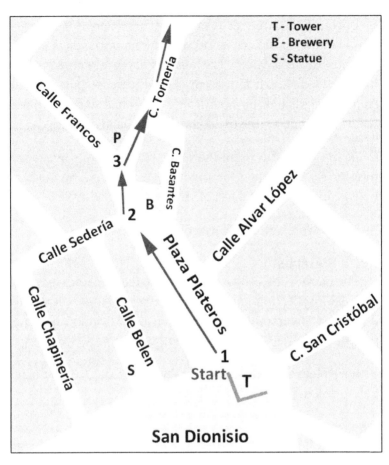

Map 8

On your right is the Torre de la Atalaya.

Torre de la Atalaya

The tower is not actually part of the San Dionisio church although it is attached to it. It was built after the church and is a watchtower and housed the town's clock.

During the sixteenth century, Moors from North Africa often landed on the coast and would kidnap the local people for ransom or slavery. The villages along the coast would light a signal fire if any Moorish boats were spotted. The smoke would then be seen from the Watchtower and Jerez would send out a force to defend the village in danger.

At the time of writing there are plans afoot to make the interior safe and open the tower up to visitors. So perhaps when you visit you will be able to climb up for the view.

The Tower overlooks Plaza Plateros

Plaza Plateros

The name of this square has changed many times over the centuries, reflecting how it was used at the time. Currently it's called Silversmiths Square from the Silversmiths Guild which stood here in the seventeenth century.

It's a pleasant little tree-lined square which is a good place for a drink in the evening.

Map 8.1 - With the tower behind you, walk down the length of the square towards a pink building which you will see at the other end of the square.

Beer fans might want to have a look in the Gorilla micro-brewery which is installed there at the time of writing.

Map 8.2 - With the square now behind you, and the pink building on your right, walk straight ahead along orange tree-lined Calle Tornería.

As you reach the last orange tree you will see a fork in the road where Calle Torneria continues off to the right and Calle Francos leads off to the left.

There is plaque on the building which stands between the two streets – it sits just to the left of the iron balcony. It has an image of a book on it and it commemorates Joaquin Portillo.

Joaquin Portillo

He came from Jerez. His trade was bookselling and the building the plaque is on was his shop. He made good use of the books which passed through his hands, studying and learning about the world and the arts. He thought everyone should have access to knowledge, so he not only sold books, but held discussion groups in the bookstore and rented books out to those who could never afford to buy them.

He fell foul of the authorities who accused him of holding illegal political meetings. As a consequence he was exiled. Whilst in exile he wrote "Jerez Nights", an extensive record of the history and buildings of Jerez. It was published in 1839 by the Juan Mellen printing shop on Plaza de Plateros, and has proved invaluable to historians today as they try to piece together what the city looked like long ago.

Sadly he died in poverty, but in 1996 Jerez rightly commemorated him with this plaque placed on his old bookshop.

Map 8.3 - With the plaque in front of you, take the road on the right hand of the fork to stay on Calle Torneria.

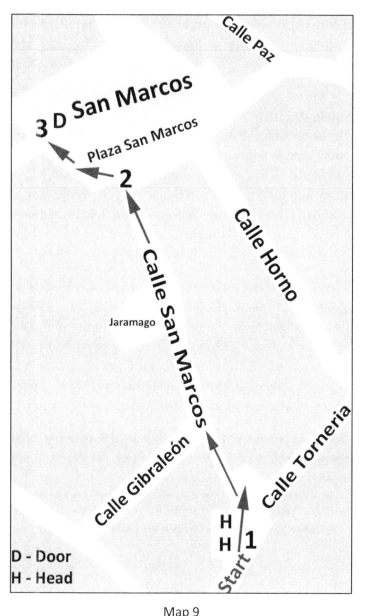

Map 9

Heads

The road will widen. Pause to take a look at the building on your left.

It has a balcony which is supported by two heads. One is thought to be a Moor wearing a turban and the other is thought to be a North American wearing a feather headdress. Jerez used to have many more examples of heads holding up balconies but many have been lost.

Map 9.1 – Just in front of you is another fork in the road. This time take the narrower left-hand street which is called Calle San Marcos.

The road will stay narrow and twist. You will pass Calle Gibraleón on your left, followed by a little square also on your left called Plaza Jaramago.

Keep walking along Calle San Marcos and you will eventually reach Plaza San Marcos, and the side of a church of the same name.

Map 9.2 - Turn left to go round the church to reach the front door.

San Marcos

This church is another of the original six churches built by Alfonso X.

Like many others it has amazingly ornate star vaulting, so if you manage to get in, make sure you look up to see it above the altar.

The altar itself is a huge golden depiction of various scenes from the Bible.

The brotherhood in this church are called "The Brotherhood of the Holy Supper", and they have their own sacred statues which are taken around Jerez on Holy days. One of them is a statue of Jesus which is called "Our Father Jesus of the Holy Supper".

Map 9.3 – Exit the church. With the door of the church behind you, turn left to walk round the church corner and back into Plaza San Marco.

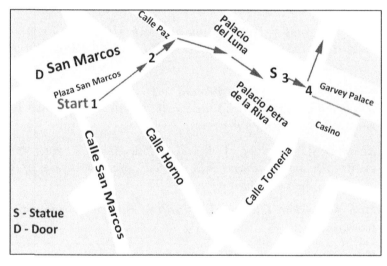

Map 10

Map 10.1 – Walk to the end of the church and pass a little street on your left which is called Plaza Nuestro Padre Jesús de la Sagrada Cena - Our Father Jesus of the Holy Supper.

Map 10.2 – Walk straight ahead, passing Calle Paz on your left. The road will bend right and take you into Plaza de Rafael Rivero.

Plaza de Rafael Rivero

This square was the first place the conquering King Alfonso X saw as he entered Jerez through the Puerta de Sevilla. Sadly that gate was demolished in the nineteenth century.

Mayor Rafael Rivero

The square is now named after Mayor Rafael Rivero and his statue stands at the edge of the square.

He brought many modern innovations and improvements to Jerez, including an aqueduct and the railway. Also with the help of the Count of Villacreces he created the Jerez Savings Bank which was the first savings bank in Spain. So Rivero is highly thought of and well-deserves his statue and his square.

Map 10.3 - Stand face to face with Rafael. The building on your left is the Palacio Petra de la Riva.

Palacio Petra de la Riva

It has a stately doorway with columns on either side and with two statues at the top. If the doors are open you can peep into the beautiful courtyard. It was the home of the Count of Villacreces who together with Refael Rivero created the Jerez savings bank.

Return to stand face-to-face with Rafael. The building behind the statue and at the far end of the square is the Palacio del Luna.

Palacio de Luna (Palace of the Moon)

This has another grand doorway topped with a lovely balcony and the family coat of arms. Don't miss the splendid sundial on the top right corner of the façade. It has the year 1777 on it – the year the palace was built.

Behind you is the Garvey Palace and next to that is what was once a casino – both now luxury hotels.

Map 10.4 - Stand facing the same direction as Rafael Rivero and walk towards the Garvey Palace hotel. Then turn left to walk along Calle Torneria.

You will reach a junction with a fountain in the middle.

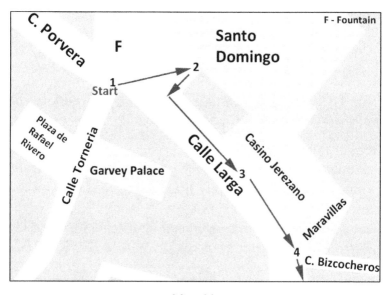

Map 11

The Fountain

The fountain is decorated with a modern statue - Jesus is on the cross and is surrounded by monks, one is wearing the traditional tall hood. The hooded monk is a bit unsettling, but the statue does depict a common enough sight on Jerez's holy days.

Map 11.1 - Across the junction, to your right, you will see a large church – one of the highlights of your trip to Jerez. Cross the road carefully to reach it.

Real Convento de Santo Domingo

After the conquest of Jerez the Dominican monks were allowed to open a monastery in an existing building which stood here outside the Seville Gate.

It wasn't the safest place, as Jerez stood on the border between the Christian and Moorish kingdoms, and attacks were not uncommon. Eventually though the Christians pushed the Moors back and Jerez started to expand beyond its old walls. The Dominican monastery became wealthy and a new monastery complex was built.

All was well until Spain started to confiscate the monasteries and convents in the nineteenth century. The church which sits beside the monastery was left, but the beautiful cloister and monastery were sold off. Fortunately it was bought by one of the wealthy sherry families who kept it more or less intact. Finally it became the property of Jerez council who closed it, renovated it, and reopened it again for everyone to enjoy. The entrance is to the right of the church door.

Do visit it if possible, as it has a beautiful Gothic cloister – the arches found in the walls which surround the central courtyard are decorated with delicate tracery. Many say it's the most beautiful cloister in Andalusia.

Map 11.2 - When you exit the church, stand with the main door behind you and walk straight ahead to reach the roadside. Turn left to walk into Calle Larga which is the main shopping street of Jerez.

After about 100 metres you will reach Casino Jerezano on your left.

Casino Jerezano

The casino has just surfaced from a recent restoration which had been needed as the stonework had deteriorated badly. Look up to see the beautiful stonework which has been repaired.

At the time of writing the Casino Jerezano is home to a bank.

Map 11.3 – Continue along Calle Larga to reach Calle Bizcochero on your left. The curved building on the corner of this street is the old Maraviallas Cinema.

Maravillas Cinema

The Maravillas cinema chain left Jerez in 1998 as the digital and streaming age arrived leaving the cinemas empty.

Unlike other cinemas which have disappeared completely, Jerez decided to keep the curved façade of the Maravillas building as a reminder. You will get a better view of it shortly.

Map 11.4 - Cross Calle Bizcocheros.

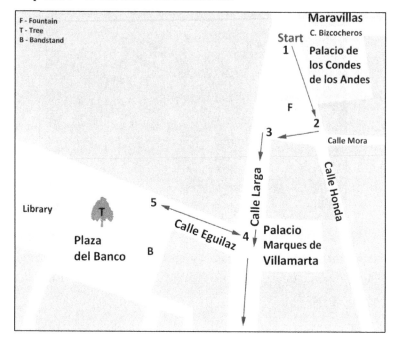

Map 12

Map 12.1 - Continue along Calle Large and you will reach the Rotonda de Los Casinos, a roundabout with a large basin fountain.

Casino Roundabout is not an official name, it's a nickname given by the locals because of the many casinos which once surrounded it – but they are all gone now.

Map 12.2 - Behind the fountain is a fork in the road. Make your way to the right hand side of the fork which is Calle Larga

Before you move away from the Rotonda de Los Casinos completely, glance back to see the old cinema building, the two beautiful old palaces on either side of it, and of course the fountain. The palace nearest you once belonged to the Count of the Andes – you may have visited the other palace which is the family home on Walk 1.

Map 12.3 - Now make your way down the right-hand side of pedestrianised Calle Larga.

After about 50 metres you will see the beautiful Palacio Marques de Villamarta on the left-hand side of the street.

Palacio Marques de Villamarta

For centuries this was the Villamarta family home. You might recognise that name – it is the same family who built the Teatro Villamarta which you saw near the start of this walk. The palace has a beautiful façade - look up to see the intricate stone carving which runs along the roof edge.

At the time of writing it's home to a fashion chain.

Map 12.4 - Stand with the palace behind you and walk straight ahead into Calle Equilaz. This will take you into Plaza del Banco.

Plaza del Banco

This square was where the Convent of San Cristobal once stood. However it had been more or less abandoned by the church and was left in ruins. It was decided to demolish it and this square was constructed in its place

The "Square of Banks" got its name from the many banks which once filled its sides. The Bank of Spain stood in the large building at the other end of the square. It is now the municipal library and it's said to be haunted by an old man dressed in military uniform and a girl dressed in white.

The banks are all gone now but this is still a lovely square with a little bandstand at one end of it, and again you might find some music filling the air.

There is also an impressive tree towering over the square. Its official name is Ficus rubiginosa and it is native to Australia. The peculiar growths which are hanging down from the tree are actually roots. In the wild they would eventually reach the ground and take root, giving the tree more stability. The roots on this tree have a way to go yet!

Backtrack along Calle Equilaz to return to Calle Larga. Turn right and walk straight down Calle Larga.

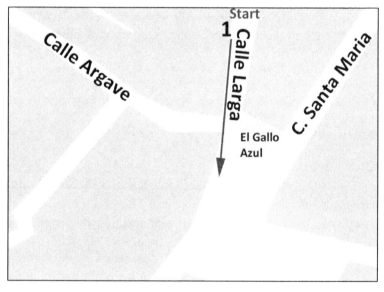

Map 13

Map 13.1 - After about 200 metres you will reach the El Gallo Azul building on your left.

You have now reached the end of this walk.

You might think about popping into El Gaoo Azul for a well-deserved refreshment if you haven't already visited.

If you want to get back to Plaza del Arenal, stand with El Gallo Azul directly behind you.

Walk straight ahead, past the signpost, and down pedestrianised Calle Lancaria. 120 metres will take you into Plaza del Arenal once more.

Walk 3 - The Old Town

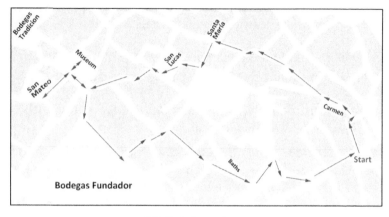

Walk 3 Overview

This walk takes you from Plaza de la Asunción on a meandering trail through the little narrow streets of old Jerez.

There are no major tourist sites to see, and it has a quite different atmosphere to the other parts of Jerez you may have already walked through. You will see churches sprinkled through the narrow streets and perhaps get an idea of just how important the church was to the people who lived here long ago.

Parts of this area are, at the time of writing, rather run-down, but Jerez has plans for restoration. Let's hope they do as it is very much part of Jerez's history.

It's also a chance to visit some very good bodegas!

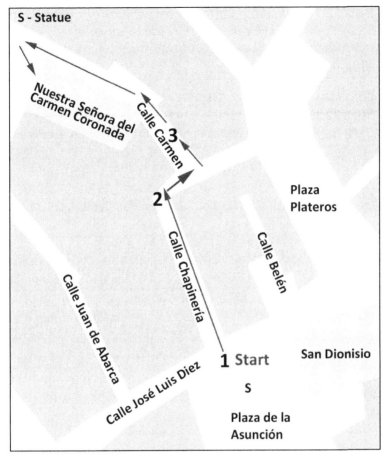

Map 1

Map 1.1 - The walk starts in Plaza de la Asunción which you may have already visited on walk 2.

Stand in the square in front of the statue with the church of San Dionisio on your right. Walk straight ahead into narrow Calle Chapinería .

Map 1.2 - The road will bend sharply right. Almost immediately after the bend, turn left into Calle Carmen.

117

Map 1.3 - Walk along Calle Carmen and after about thirty metres you will see the side of a church on your left. When you reach the end of the church, turn left to reach the church front door.

Basílica Menor de Nuestra Señora del Carmen Coronada

Helpfully the church has its name over the main doorway.

Look up above the door and you will see the Virgin in a niche which has raised curtains carved into the stone – incredibly skilful. The church has a lovely tiled mosaic at the left-hand side of the door.

Mount Carmel is in northern Israel and according to the bible it was where the Prophet Elijah headed to when he decided to become a hermit. Once there, he created an altar and he challenged the local priests of the pagan god Baal to a competition to see whose God was the best. The priests of Baal pleaded with their God to light the fire, but he wasn't listening. Step up Elijah, who asked God the same thing and Zap! the fire burst into flame.

Not surprisingly pilgrims flocked to Mount Carmel to pray in the cave said to be where Elijah lived. In the twelfth century the Carmelite order was formed at the cave after someone had a vision of the Virgin Mary there. The order soon spread all over Christian Europe.

The Carmelites arrived in Jerez soon after it was conquered by the Christians, but their first home was outside the old town wall. Some years later they moved inside the wall and built a small church on this spot. It was then replaced with this much grander church in the eighteenth century.

The church was attacked in 1931 during the "burning of convents", which started in Madrid but spread across the country. The people of Spain turned against the church and many churches and convents were set on fire.

This church survived the onslaught and was later promoted to a minor basilica by Pope Paul VI in 1968 – the pecking order of Roman Catholic churches is Cathedral, Major Basilica, Minor Basilica, church.

If the church is open, do pop in

Church Interior

The church's relatively subdued exterior doesn't prepare you for the blast of colour you will find when you step inside. Centre stage is a golden Virgin and child - both wearing glowing golden crowns. Actually Jesus was a bit of an afterthought – he was added one hundred years after the statue of Mary was installed.

The church also has a museum which was only recently opened to the public. It's mostly religious art as you would expect, but worth a look if you are interested.

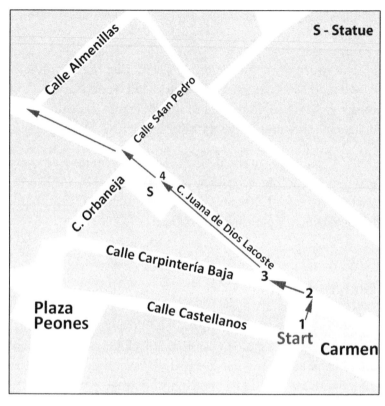

Map 2

Map 2.1 - When you want to move on, stand with the main door of the church behind you. Turn right and walk a few steps to reach the T-junction.

Map 2.2 - At the T-junction turn left and you will soon reach a fork in the road.

Map 2.3 - Take the upper right-hand street which is called Calle Juana de Dios Lacoste.

You will reach a little tree-filled square on your left. It holds a statue of Santa Angela de la Cruz surrounded by roses.

Santa Angela de la Cruz

She is a relatively new saint who came from Seville and was born in the nineteenth century.

She was a very religious young woman, and she tried hard to become a nun but was always turned down by the nunneries because of her poor health. It was then that she had a vision of Jesus on the cross, but in front of that cross stood an empty cross. She interpreted her vision as Jesus telling her to help the poor by being poor.

Out of frustration at her failure to join an order, she and three other wannabe nuns created their own religious order called The Sisters of the Company of the Cross. They dedicated themselves to helping the poor and nursing the ill. A year later they were given the official nod from the Archbishop of Seville and began to expand their order all over Andalucía.

In 1976 the process of sainthood for Angela began but it's a long process. She was finally declared a saint in 2003 by Pope John Paul II.

Map 2.4 - Stand face to face with Angela.

Turn right to leave the square by walking straight ahead along Calle Juana de Dios Lacoste, passing Calle Almanilla on your right.

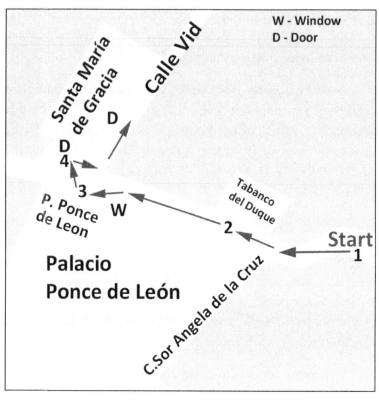

Map 3

Map 3.1 - The road will twist and turn a little now. Continue to pass Calle Sor Angela de la Cruz on your left, and then pause to have a look at the restored building on your right.

El Tabanco del Duque

Until not too long ago, this was one of the very run-down buildings which were in danger of collapse. Jerez has stepped in, saved what was saveable of the original building, and rebuilt around it.

122

It's planned to be a public space, so if it's open you can pop in to see the original stonework which was saved.

Map 3.2 - Continue along Calle Juana de Dios Lacoste and you will walk into a little square called Plaza Ponce de Leon.

Plaza Ponce de León

This little square is named after the palace that looks over it. You can spot it by the beautiful window on the corner – the only really palatial feature of the palace exterior.

The window is covered in mythical beings, swirling vegetation, and a few coats of arms; but once again Jerez needs to send in the restorers to save it as the carvings are wearing away. At the bottom of the window are two inscriptions

Omnia preterunt preter amare deum

Everything perishes except the love of God

Vanitas vanitatum et omnia vanitas

Vanity of vanities and all vanity

The palace was built in the fifteenth century by the crown, but was later given to the Esteban family for their support of King Enrique IV. Esteban's granddaughter inherited it and she married Francisco Ponce de Leon, which is where the palace and the square get their names.

Map 3.3 - Now stand in Plaza Ponce de León with the palace window on your right-hand side.

You will see a convent, decorated with a beautiful blue and yellow tiled image of the Virgin Mary, a little to the left in front of you.

Convento de Santa María de Gracia

A local lady, Dona Francisca de Trujillo, donated all her fortune including her home to found an Augustinian convent in the sixteenth century. She became its first prioress. The convent of the Sisters of the Cross has been here ever since.

It's had its ups and down. Some of the nuns marched out in rebellion in 1784 because they did not like the new Abbess. They took refuge in another convent for a year, but they did eventually return.

These days the nuns are well known for their delicious sweets which they make at Christmas time and ship all over Spain. If you are very lucky you might find the church open to have a look around.

Map 3.4 - Face the convent door and walk down the right-hand side of the convent into Calle Vid. Stop when you reach the church side door.

Calle Vid

The convent has had some restoration in recent years. Spot the two decorative arches on the church wall just past the side door.

Calle Vid Ghost

This little street is said to be haunted by a nun who died in childbirth in one of the buildings on Calle Vid.

The story tells us that one evening two men met a nun while they were walking down this street. They asked her if they could be of any assistance. The nun thanked them and asked them to follow her and help her carry a heavy sack.

They followed the nun, but she sped off, turned a corner and disappeared. The man in the lead suddenly realised that he was alone and made his way back to find the body of his friend who had had his throat slit.

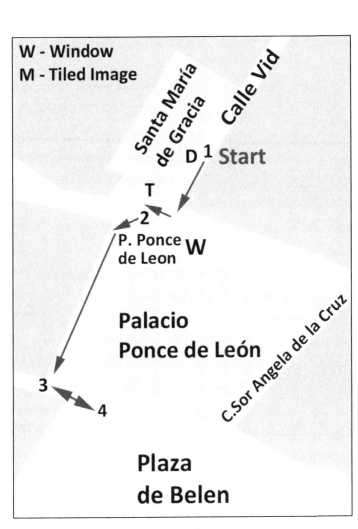

Map 4

Map 4.1 – Backtrack to stand with tiled image of the Virgin Mary behind you.

Map 4.2 - Walk straight ahead into a narrow street which unsurprisingly is called Ponce de Leon.

Map 4.3 - At its end, take a step to the left into Plaza de Belen.

You will find a huge rather ugly concrete open space, but you do get a great view of the Cathedral and the tower of the San Miguel Church.

Map 4.4 - Back-track a few steps to the junction with Ponce de Leon.

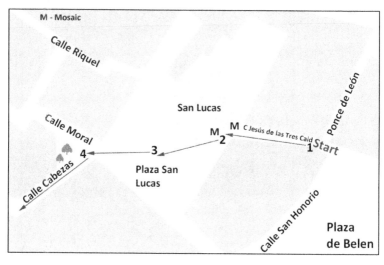

Map 5

Map 5.1 - Walk straight ahead along Calle Jesús de las Tres Caid.

Just as the street bends to the left, you will find two tiled mosaics on the wall of a church. The second mosaic is called Jesus of the Three Falls

Jesús de las Tres Caid (Jesus of the Three Falls)

It's unusual as it shows Jesus carrying the cross and he is on his knees. According to the bible Jesus stumbled three times on his way to the crucifixion, and this mosaic portrays the third fall. It also depicts a famous statue which you will find in the church if it is open.

Map 5.2 - Follow the street around the corner to reach Plaza San Lucas where you will find the church of San Lucas on your right.

San Lucas

This very elderly church was built in medieval times. It is one of six churches within the old city wall which were built over Moorish mosques just after the Christians conquered Jerez.

The church sits above the sloping plaza on a purpose built platform and at the top of a wide stairway. The bellower is not nearly as old as the church itself - it was only added in the eighteenth century. You can see its bells from the plaza and below that a sundial.

Above the main door is a niche where Saint Luke stands, and at his feet is his symbol, the ox.

The church is home to the Brotherhood of the Three Falls. If it is open do pop in to see the statue illustrated on the mosaic you just passed. It is a colourful relatively modern statue which was carved in the 1940's.

There is also a statue of the crucifixion which is called Cristo de la Salud. It is much older and sadder.

The church had become unstable over the centuries and was in danger of collapse. Fortunately the church was restored just a few years ago. During the restoration, the Brotherhood of the Three Falls found refuge with the nuns of the convent of Santa María de Gracia which you saw earlier. The brothers have now returned home and proudly carry their statues in Jerez's holy processions.

Map 5.3 - Stand with the church steps behind you and cross the square diagonally right.

Map 5.4 - You will see some trees leaning over an old wall at the corner. Leave the square by Calle Cabezas – you should have the trees on your right-hand side as you do.

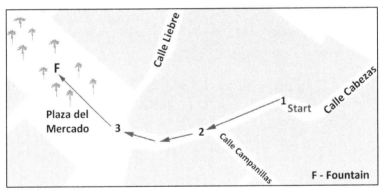

Map 6

Calle Cabezas

This is another very old street. Its name means Street of the Heads, and some think its name came from more balconies being held up by sculpted heads, like the one you saw on Walk 2. If so, none have survived.

131

Map 6.1 - Follow this wiggly street. Ignore Calle Campanillas on your left and stay on Calle Cabezas.

Map 6.2 - The street narrows before taking you into a large square with tall palm trees in the middle.

Map 6.3 - Walk over to the fountain in the middle where you will find benches to have a rest, or to the surrounding cafes for a refreshment. Decide what to do next.

Choices

You might now wish to zoom off to the Bodegas Tradicion or the Bodegas Fundador if you have pre-booked tickets and the time is right. If so, follow the instructions below to reach either bodega:

- Getting To Bodegas Tradicion is on page 133
- Getting To Bodegas Fundador is on page 135

Both bodegas routes will bring you back to Plaza del Mercado to continue.

If you do not wish to visit either bodega, continue from Plaza del Mercado on page 141 instead.

Getting To Bodegas Tradicion

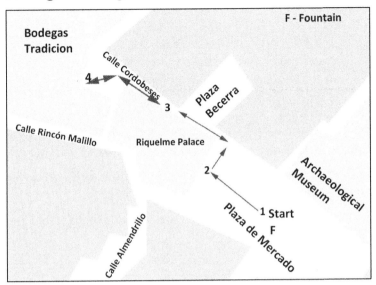

Map 7

Map 7.1 - To reach the Bodegas Tradicionm stand with the Archaeological Museum on your right.

You will see the ornate Riquelme Palace straight ahead of you. Walk towards the palace.

Map 7.2 - Go round the right-hand side of the palace. You will pass a small square on your right called Plaza Becerra.

Map 7.3 - Keep the palace wall on your left and you will walk into another little square where you will find the entrance to the Bodegas Tradicion diagonally left.

Bodegas Tradicion

Although the bodega sits in the oldest part of town, the company inside it is actually quite new. The original bodega which operated from here ceased trading, so the building was bought up, renovated, and a new sherry company was created.

The sherry and brandy you get to taste are very high quality and the added bonus is the tour of the art gallery. In it you will find works by many famous Spanish artists such as Goya, Velasquez, and Zurbaran.

Map 7.4 - When you have completed your visit, cross the square diagonally right to return along Calle Cordobeses.

Pass Plaza Becerra on your left and return to the fountain on Plaza del Mercado.

Continue exploring from Plaza de Mercado on page 141.

Getting To Bodegas Fundador

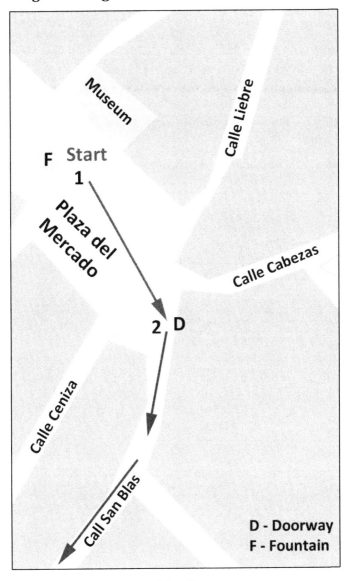

Map 8

Map 8.1 - Stand by the fountain with the museum door behind you. Turn left to reach the side of the Plaza del Mercado.

You will see a sadly neglected wall which has another ornate but elderly doorway; it sits between two bricked up smaller doors.

Map 8.2 - Face the wall and turn right to walk into Calle San Blas.

Walk straight ahead and pass Calle Ildefonso on your left.

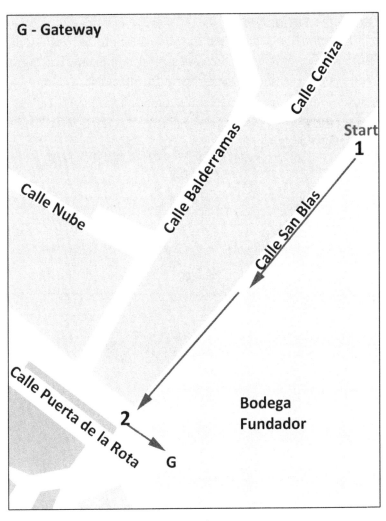

Map 9

Map 9.1 – Continue along Calle San blass to reach a T-junction with busy Calle Puerta de la Rota.

Map 9.2 - Turn left and walk straight ahead to reach the gate of Bodegas Fundador.

Bodegas Fundador

This bodega was started in the eighteenth century by the Domecq family, and is the oldest and handsomest in Jerez. You get to taste sherry in the beautiful old cloister.

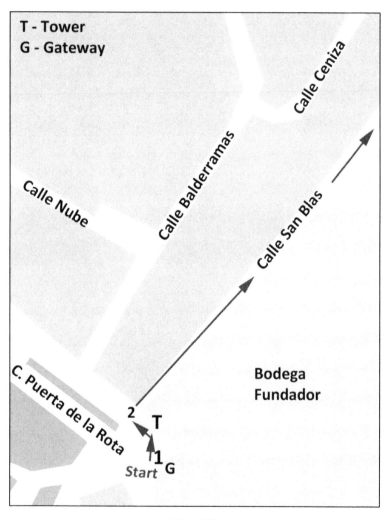

Map 10

Map 10.1 - When you have completed your visit, retrace a few steps along Calle Puerta de Rota.

Riquelme Tower

As you do, don't miss the very old Riquelme Tower on your right. The tower is now incorporated into the Fundador Bodegas building.

Historians have speculated that it was originally part of the old city wall. You will see what's left of the Riquelme Palace later.

The tower has recently been restored and there are plans to give tours to visitors, so fingers crossed it will be open when you visit.

Map 10.2 – Facing the tower door take a few steps to your left. Then take the next right into Calle San Blas.

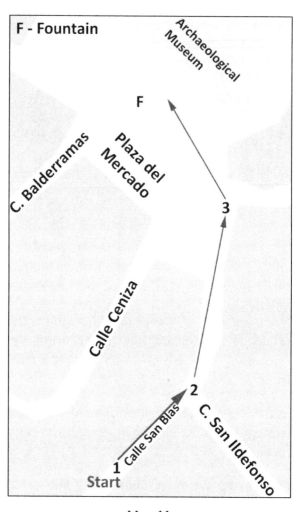

Map 11

Map 11.1 – Continue along Calle San Blas.

Map 11.2 - After about 200 metres you will pass Calle San Ildefonso on the right. Keep walking and you will find yourself back in Plaza del Mercado.

Map 11.3 - Return to the Fountain.

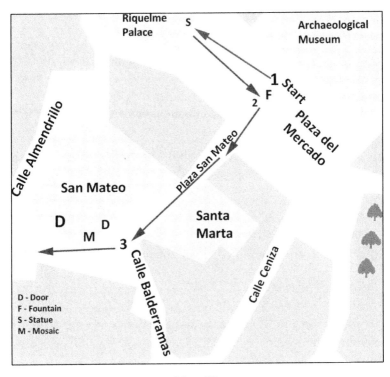

Map 12

Plaza del Mercado

This square was the centre of old Jerez when the Moors ruled the city. Market Square gets its name because this used to be where the Moorish market (the souk) once stood. Many centuries later it was where executions took place.

The Black Hand

You read about the trials of The Black Hand on Walk 1. Of the 15 people who were sentenced to death by the Jerez court, eight were executed in this square in 1884. The other seven had their sentences commuted to life imprisonment.

Exploring the Market Area

There are a couple of sites to see around the Market Square before moving on; the Archaeological Museum, the Riquelme Palace, and the San Mateo and Santa Marta churches.

Archaeological Museum

If you have time you could visit the archaeological museum. It sits on one side of the square and has Museo Arqueologico above the door. The ticket price includes an audio guide which makes the whole visit much more interesting and worthwhile. If that doesn't appeal, continue this walk from "Riquelme Palace" on page 146.

Inside the Museum

Inside you can trace the fascinating history of Jerez, from its pre-history to the Romans and the Moors, via the artefacts which have been excavated and lovingly preserved. Here are some favourites to find.

Marble Idols

One of the most fascinating items are these little marble idols with captivating eyes and raised eyebrows from about 2,500 BC.

Greek Helmet

This ancient bronze helmet was only discovered in 1938, on the banks of the Guadalete River which lies north east of Jerez. It's a Corinthian helmet from about 700 BC.

This type of helmet was designed to fully cover the warrior's head but as you can see, the eyes, nose and, mouth were left alarmingly undefended.

Roman Sarcophagus

This artefact was found in the seventeenth century, and since then it has been damaged. So what you see has been pieced back together, using a drawing of the original from the eighteenth century as a guide. It's quite easy to spot the original seven fragments. It's so sad that so little of it has survived.

Bowl with Stag

This beautiful item is from the time of the Moors and is from the tenth century. In the middle of the bowl is a green stag holding a branch in its mouth.

145

When you have finished browsing, head back into the sunshine.

Riquelme Palace

Map 12.1- With the archaeological museum door behind you, turn right and walk to the end of the square to reach the Riquelme Palace.

This palace belonged to the Riquelme family and it was built here, in the heart of old Jerez, to show off that family's wealth and power.

It was constructed in the sixteenth century and the architect used the very latest ideas in design – all to impress the other powerful families in Jerez. The family coat of arms is just above the doorway, held by two bearded men.

However the fortunes of the Riquelme family faded and their palace was abandoned for centuries. In the end Jerez city council took it under its wing.

Hercules

Hercules

Nemean lion

Neso and Deyanira

You can see that the palace is covered with various mythological figures. The two large figures show Hercules in action wielding a club. Directly below them are two panels, each telling part of the story of Hercules.

Hercules and Deyanira

The panel on the left shows Hercules executing one of his Twelve Tasks - defeating the Nemean lion which had impenetrable skin. That story has already been mentioned in Walk 2.

The panel on the right shows his wife Deyanira being abducted by the centaur Neso. We see Hercules firing a poisoned arrow at Neso, fatally wounding him.

The tale goes on to tell us that as Neso lay dying, he convinced Deyanira that his blood could be used on Hercules to make sure he never left her. She believed him and later

147

smeared it on her husband's shirt. Hercules put the shirt on and the toxic blood burned through him. Knowing he was dying, Hercules built a funeral pyre for himself and died on it. Deyanira realised what she had done and killed herself.

Virgil's Aeneid

One of the better preserved figures is just to the left of the blocked-up doorway. It's a woman's face surrounded by the words "Camila Regina Magna". She is a character from Virgil's Aeneid who was raised by her father to be a warrior. She was an enemy of the story's hero, Aeneas, and she died in the tale.

At the time of writing the palace is unused, but there are discussions of moving the art collection from the Bodegas Tradicion into it, so you may be able to buy a ticket and explore inside when you visit.

Map 12.2 - Return to the fountain in Market Square.

With the museum door behind you, walk across the square into Plaza San Mateo.

When the street opens up, you will find the large San Mateo church on your right.

San Mateo

This gothic church is one of the six churches built after the Christian conquest. Stand back and look up to see its bell-tower and three bells. At the left side of the church door is a tiled image of "Our Lord of Sorrows".

The church has recently been restored, so if it's open go inside to see the towering golden retablo which sits behind the main altar. As you approach it, don't forget to look up to see the wonderful stone vaulting.

Map 12.3 – Face the door of San Mateo. Turn left to go round the left hand side of the church into a little triangular plaza.

Here you will find another ornate church doorway that has been bricked up. The reason was the Lisbon Earthquake in 1755, which was so devastating that its tremors reached as far as Jerez and this side of the church was badly damaged. The door was sealed to stabilise the church.

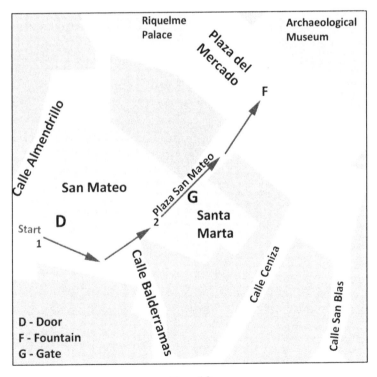

Map 13

Map 13.1 - Backtrack around the corner of the church to return to Plaza San Mateo.

Opposite San Mateo church you will see the bright orange gateway and the iron gate of Santa Marta

Santa Marta

This is the headquarters of the Brotherhood of Santa Marta. They are relative newcomers to the brotherhoods of Jerez, as they were only formed in 1958 and were originally based in San Mateo. They moved across the square in 1997 into a new chapel of their own.

Like most brotherhoods they take their treasured statues on a holy procession around Jerez every year. They have two, one of Santa Marta herself and the other of Jesus being carried to his tomb. Santa Marta is the patron saint of housewives, waiters and waitresses.

Map 13.2 - Face the orange gateway of Santa Marta and turn left to return to Plaza del Mercado.

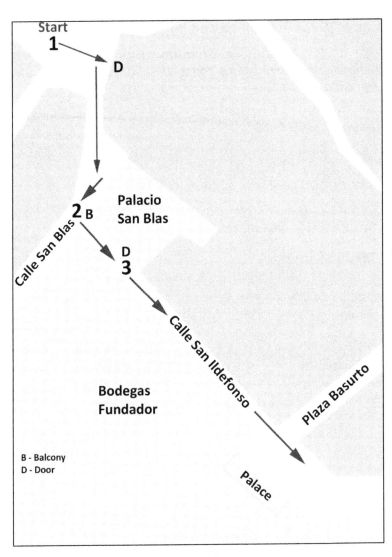

Start
1
D

2 B
Palacio
San Blas
D
3

Calle San Blas

Calle San Ildefonso

Bodegas
Fundador

Plaza Basurto

B - Balcony
D - Door

Palace

Map 14

Leave Plaza del Mercado

Map 14.1 – Stand by the fountain with the museum door behind you. Turn left to reach the side of the Plaza del Mercado.

You will see a sadly neglected wall which has another ornate but elderly doorway; it sits between two bricked up smaller doors.

Face the wall and turn right to walk into Calle San Blas.

Stop when the street widens into a little triangular plaza; on your left is the Palacio San Blas.

Palacio San Blas

At the time of writing, the palace is another of Jerez's neglected palaces and it is in a sorry state. There is talk of it becoming a hotel, so with luck you may see it restored.

It was owned by José Domecq de la Riva of the Domecq sherry family. He was a colourful character whose nickname was El Pantera, The Panther, perhaps because he kept a panther in a cage in the palace.

It has a couple of colourful images on the exterior and an ornate iron corner balcony. If you could enter the palace you would find a tile which is inscribed with:

Visitors are as welcome when they arrive as when they leave

Another tile says philosophically:

Good life is expensive, there is another cheaper but it is not good

Map 14.2 - Take the next left into Calle San Ildefonso.

Not too far along on your left you will see the door to the Palacio San Blas chapel – it has some greenery from the garden tumbling over the wall above it.

The chapel was built by the Domecq family as a stand-in while the nearby San Mateo church was being repaired after the Lisbon Earthquake.

Map 14.3 - Continue downhill along Calle San Ildefonso with the buildings of Bodegas Fundador on your right.

You can probably smell the sherry as you pass the Bodegas doors.

Pause when the road widens out, and you see a very handsome palace on your right behind iron railings.

Calle San Ildefonso

This road at one time was where many of Jerez's wealthiest families lived. However in the seventeenth century they started to move to other parts of Jerez and no-one moved in to replace them. The grand buildings were simply abandoned and left to the elements.

This whole street was bought up by the Domecq family in the nineteenth century, and they have been involved in its total renovation. It is now a striking contrast to some of the other streets you have been walking along.

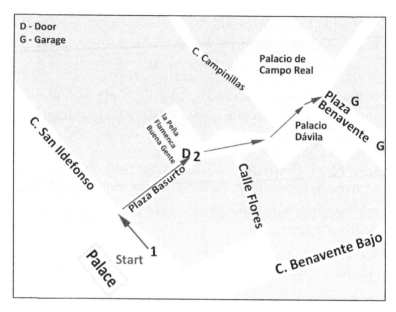

D - Door
G - Garage

C. Campinillas

Palacio de
Campo Real

Plaza Benavente

Palacio Dávila

G

G

la Peña Flamenca Buena Gente

C. San Ildefonso

Plaza Basurto

D 2

Calle Flores

Palace

Start 1

C. Benavente Bajo

Map 15

Map 15.1 – Turn so that the palace is now on your left-hand side. Walk back uphill a few steps and turn right into Calle Basurto.

You will reach another grand door on your left-hand side; it belongs to the Palacio de Basurto.

Flamenco and la Peña Flamenca Buena Gente

Seville claims to be the home of flamenco; however those in the know agree that Jerez is the true birthplace of this intrinsically Andalusian dance. Flamenco is still part of everyday culture in this city, and not just for the tourists.

A Peña is a flamenco association where shows are staged for the love of the dance and the music. There are about 15 of them scattered around Jerez. No fee is charged to the audience, although there will be a suggestion of a donation to keep the place going.

A bit of luck is involved in finding a performance which will fit in with your plans. If you are in town when the annual flamenco festival is on, you will find performances everywhere. Otherwise you need to know where to go to see it. Here is one possibility.

La Peña Flamenca Buena Gente has recently relocated into the Palacio de Basurto. So if you would like to see a "real" flamenco show, take a look here to see what is on during your visit.

Map 15.2 – With the door behind you, turn left to continue into a little square called Plaza Basurto.

Walk diagonally right to cross the square, ignoring Calle Flores on your right.

You will walk into Plaza Benavente which is has some ugly garages on it, but you will also find two old palaces.

Palacio de Campo Real

The palace on your left was a gift from Alonso X to another of his trusted knights who fought beside him in the battle to take Jerez. The palace was built in 1545 on top of another old Moorish building.

Inside is very beautiful; filled with tapestries, paintings, and other treasures. It also has lovely gardens and is a popular wedding spot.

Tours are available but only between 11 am and 1pm, so you may have to revisit if you wish to see inside.

There is another smaller palace sitting on the square.

Palacio Dávila

This palace was built by Bartolomé Núñez Dávila in the early 16th century. It has handsome double columns on either side of the door, but its most decorative feature is the beautiful corner window and balcony.

Enjoy its lovely exterior, because this palace was "reformed" last century and the inside bears no resemblance to its former self. The architects basically tore the inside apart and converted it into apartments for disadvantaged families. Since then the interior has simply deteriorated and the tenants who still live there are waiting for Jerez to fix things.

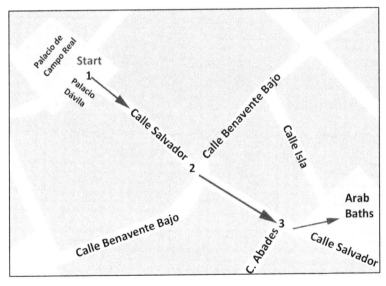

Map 16

Map 16.1 - Face the Palacio Dávila and turn left to leave the square along narrow Calle Salvador.

Map 16.2 – You will reach a staggered crossroads with Calle Benavente Bajo. Walk straight ahead staying on Calle Salvador.

Map 16.3 – Pass Calle Abades on your right and you will reach a triangular crossroads.

On your left at number 6 stands a luxurious townhouse from the eighteenth century, and inside is Arab Baths Hammam Andalusi

Arab Baths Hammam Andalusi

Entering this establishment is like taking a step into the past. Think of Moorish decoration, pools of water, subdued lighting, mint tea, and massage. If you would like to enjoy the experience you must make a booking.

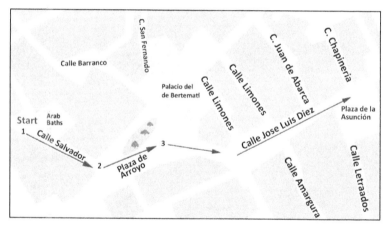

Map 17

Back into town

Map 17.1 - Stand with the bath house behind you and turn left.

Walk downhill on Calle Salvador to reach Plaza del Arroya which you may have already visited on Walk 1.

Map 17.2- Turn left to pass the little tree-filled garden.

Map 17.3 – Walk straight ahead uphill on Calle José Luis Diez.

After about 200 metres you will find Plaza de la Asunción on your right where this walk ends.

Did you enjoy these walks?

I do hope you found these walks both fun and interesting, and I would love feedback. If you have any comments, either good or bad, please review this book

You could also drop me a line on my amazon web page.

Other Strolling Around Books to try:

- Strolling Around Bilbao
- Strolling Around Arles
- Strolling Around Bruges
- Strolling Around Ghent
- Strolling Around Verona
- Strolling Around Palma
- Strolling Around Ljubljana
- Strolling Around Berlin
- Strolling Around The Hague
- Strolling Around Porto
- Strolling Around Lucca
- Strolling Around Amsterdam
- Strolling Around Madrid
- Strolling Around Lisbon
- Strolling Around Sienna
- Strolling Around Delft
- Strolling Around Florence
- Strolling Around Toledo
- Strolling Around Bath
- Strolling Around Antwerp
- Strolling Around Pisa

Printed in Great Britain
by Amazon

33872325R00089